access to sociology

CULTURE
and
IDENTITY

David Abbott

Series Editor: Paul Selfe

Hodder & Stoughton

A MEMBER OF THE HODDER HEADLINE GROUP

DEDICATION

For Christopher and Olivia, who will have to face the challenges and stresses of late capitalism.

Order queries: please contact Bookpoint Ltd, 39 Milton Park, Abingdon, Oxon OX14 4TD. Telephone: (44) 01235 400414, Fax: (44) 01235 400454. Lines are open from 9.00–6.00, Monday to Saturday, with a 24 hour message answering service. Email address: orders@bookpoint.co.uk

A catalogue record for this title is available from The British Library

ISBN 0 340 711833

First published 1998
Impression number 10   9   8   7   6   5   4   3
Year   2004   2003   2002   2001

Cover photo from Zefa Picture Library (UK) Ltd

Typeset by Transet Limited, Coventry, England.
Printed in Great Britain for Hodder & Stoughton Educational, a division of Hodder Headline plc, 338 Euston Road, London NW1 3BH by Redwood Books, Trowbridge, Wilts.

CONTENTS

ACKNOWLEDGEMENTS

Contrary to popular opinion writing is not an entirely solitary process, and I have to thank many people for their part in helping this book come into being. Firstly I have to thank my family, and especially Rosie, for tolerating my obsessions and absences. I have also to thank Elisabeth Tribe for starting the project and getting me involved, whilst Anna Clark and Llinos Edwards have been extremely patient and helpful in ensuring that it was completed. Paul Selfe provided support and help which went well beyond the call of duty.

I also wish to thank colleagues and students at Hills Road Sixth Form College, Cambridge; space does not permit the comprehensive listing so desired by my star-struck students, but they know who they are. My colleagues Brian Harney and Dr Peter Holmes have been extremely supportive, and Christine Gynane ensured that I had a supply of up to date articles. Thanks also has to go to numerous colleagues in the sociological community: Tony Lawson, Pete Langley, Hugh Chignell, Warren Kidd, and Paul Manning have all given advice and encouragement at various times. The responsibility for what is written lies, as always, with the author.

The publishers would like to thank the following for permission to reproduce copyright photographs:
Adam Woolfitt/Corbis, p 70, top; Owen Franken/Corbis, p 70, bottom; US Department of Defense/Corbis, p 81; Bryn Colton, Assignments Photographers/ Corbis, p 110; Macduff Everton/Corbis, p 122.

1

INTRODUCTION

HOW TO USE THE BOOH

EACH CHAPTER IN this book examines one or more of the central debates relating to sociology. The text is devised for readers with little or no background knowledge in the subject, and there are Study Points and Activities throughout to encourage a consideration of the issues raised. Student readers are advised to make use of these and answer them either on paper or in group discussion, a particularly fruitful way of learning; they will assist them to develop the skills of interpretation, analysis and evaluation. There are many ways of preparing for an exam, but a thorough understanding of the material is obviously crucial.

Each chapter is structured to give a clear understanding of the authors, concepts and issues that you need to know about. To assist understanding and facilitate later revision, it is often helpful to make concise notes.

MAKING NOTES FROM THE BOOK

Linear notes
- Bold headings establish key points: names, theories and concepts.
- Subheadings indicate details of relevant issues.
- A few numbered points list related arguments.

Diagram or pattern notes
- Use a large blank sheet of paper and write a key idea in the centre.
- Make links between this and related issues.
- Show also the connections between sub issues which share features in common.

Both systems have their advantages and disadvantages, and may take some time to perfect. Linear notes can be little more than a copy of what is already in the book and patterned notes can be confusing. But if you practise the skill, they can reduce material efficiently and concisely becoming invaluable for revision. Diagrammatic notes may be very useful for those with a strong visual memory and provide a clear overview of a whole issue, showing patterns of interconnection. The introduction of helpful drawings or a touch of humour into the format is often a good way to facilitate the recall of names, research studies and complex concepts.

Activity

- Make a diagram to show the two ways of making notes with their possible advantages and disadvantages

SKILLS ADVICE

Students must develop and display certain skills for their examination and recognise which ones are being tested in a question. The clues are frequently in key words in the opening part. The skill domains are:

1 **Knowledge and understanding:** the ability to discuss the views of the main theorists; their similarities and differences; the strengths and weaknesses of evidence. To gain marks students must display this when asked to *explain, examine, suggest a method, outline reasons*.
2 **Interpretation, application and analysis:** the use of evidence in a logical, relevant way, either to show how it supports arguments or refutes them. Students must show this ability when asked *identify, use items A/B/C, draw conclusions from a table*.
3 **Evaluation:** the skill of assessing evidence in a balanced way so that logical conclusions follow. Students can recognise this skill when asked to *assess, critically examine, comment on levels of reliability, compare and contrast*, or if asked to *what extent*.

Activity

Draw an evaluation table, as below, using the whole of an A4 page. Examine studies as you proceed in your work and fill in the relevant details. Keep it for revision purposes.

Sociologist		
Title of the study	Strengths	Weaknesses
Verdict		
Judgement/justification		

REVISION ADVICE

- Keep clear notes at all times in a file or on disk (with back up copy).
- Be familiar with exam papers and their demands.
- Become familiar with key authors, their theories, their research and sociological concepts.

Activity
Make and keep **Key Concept Cards**, as shown below.

COLLECTIVE CONSCIENCE

Key idea

A term used by **Durkheim** meaning:

- The existence of a social and moral order exterior to individuals and acting upon them as an independent force.
- The shared sentiments, beliefs and values of individuals which make up the **collective conscience.**
- In **traditional societies** it forms the basis of social order.
- As societies modernise the collective conscience weakens: **mechanical solidarity** is replaced by **organic solidarity**.

Key theorist: Emile Durkheim

Syllabus area: Sociological Theories of Religion: Functionalism

EXAMINATION ADVICE

To develop an effective method of writing, answers should be:

- **Sociological:** use the language and research findings of sociologists; do not use anecdotal opinion gathered from people not involved in sociology to support arguments.

- **Adequate in length:** enough is written to obtain the marks available.
- **Interconnected** with other parts of the syllabus (such as stratification, gender, ethnicity).
- **Logical:** the answer follows from the relevant evidence.
- **Balanced:** arguments and counter arguments are weighed; references are suitable.
- **Accurate:** reliable data is obtained from many sources.

The three skill areas on p 2 should be demonstrated, so that the question is answered effectively.

In displaying knowledge, the student is not necessarily also demonstrating interpretation.

- This must be specified with phrases like 'Therefore, this study leads to the view that...'
- Sections of answers should hang together, one leading to the next. This shows how the question is being answered by a process of analysis based on the evidence.
- Reach a conclusion based on the evidence used and the interpretations made.

The skill of evaluation is often regarded (not necessarily accurately) as the most problematic. Evaluation means being judge and jury; the strengths and weaknesses of evidence is assessed and an overall judgement about its value is made. To evaluate an argument or theory, consider whether it usefully opens up debate; explains the events studied; does it have major weaknesses?

Activity
Look through some past examination papers and pick out the evaluation questions. Underline the evaluation words and work out which skills are required.

COURSEWORK ADVICE

Coursework provides an opportunity to carry out a study using primary and/or secondary data to investigate an issue of sociological interest, and must address theoretical issues. The suggestions included at the end of each chapter may be adapted or used to generate further ideas. Final decision must be agreed with a teacher or tutor.

MAKING A PLAN

Before starting a piece of coursework, you should make a plan:

1 Read and make notes from articles describing research projects in journals.
2 Have a clear aim in mind; choose an issue that interests you and is within your ability.
3 Decide more precisely what you want to know; establish a simple hypothesis to test.
4 Select a range of possible methods; consider both quantitative and qualitative. You may find it useful to conduct a pilot study.
5 Decide on a range of possible sources of information.
6 List the people to whom you can seek help, perhaps including a statistician.

WRITING THE PROJECT

1 Seek frequent advice from a teacher or tutor.
2 Check the weighting for different objectives in the marking scheme.
3 Keep clear notes throughout, including new ideas and any problems that arise.
4 Limit its length to between 3–5,000 words. Check your exam board requirements.
5 Check with your teacher to find out how your study should be set out. You may need to use one of the following lists of headings, depending on which syllabus you are studying:
   a **Rationale:** a reason for choosing the subject; preliminary observations on the chosen area.
   b **Context:** an outline of the theoretical and empirical context of the study.
   c **Methodology:** a statement of the methodology used and reasons for selecting it.
   d **Content:** presentation of the evidence and/or argument including results.
   e **Evaluation:** the outcomes are weighed and strengths and weaknesses noted.
   f **Sources:** all the sources of information are listed.

OR

   a **Title**
   b **Contents**
   c **Abstract:** a brief summary of the aims, methods, findings and evaluation.
   d **Rationale**
   e **The Study**
   f **Research Diary**
   g **Bibliography**
   h **Appendix:** to include proposal for the study, single examples of a questionnaire or other data-gathering instrument and transcripts of interviews.
   i **Annex:** to incude raw data gathered.

Paul Selfe
Series editor

2

CULTURE, IDENTITY AND SOCIETY

Introduction

THIS CHAPTER EXAMINES why sociologists criticise purely biological accounts of human behaviour, and examines sociologists' claims about how we learn to be members of society. This involves understanding what sociologists mean by the concepts of culture, identity and socialisation.

Sociology has always been concerned with understanding how individuals are influenced by larger forces, such as class, ethnicity, gender and age. To many, these aspects of our lives seem to be natural forces, which we can do little to change – such as the process of ageing. However, to sociologists, all of these forces are socially constructed. By this, sociologists mean that they are learnt.

Table 1: *Concepts and issues in this chapter*	
KEY CONCEPTS	KEY ISSUES
● Sociobiology	Why are contemporary sociologists so interested in culture and identity?
● Culture	
● Identity	
● Norms	What are culture and identity?
● Values	
● Socialisation	Do sociologists agree on how to define them?
● Definitions of culture	

NATURE OR NURTURE – SOCIOLOGY VERSUS SOCIOBIOLOGY

In studying society, sociologists aim to show how the actions of individuals are affected by wider social forces, such as class, ethnicity and gender, and by social institutions, such as governments, schools, banks, factories, etc. One of the key concepts which sociologists use in illustrating these influences is culture. The importance of the concept becomes clear when contrasted with the view of the theorists known as sociobiologists.

Sociobiologists argue that human behaviour can be explained in terms of inherited behaviour. This involves seeing behaviour as natural, and sociobiologists would want to explain for example, the differences in male and female behaviour in terms of natural differences. Male behaviour would be seen as being naturally more aggressive, since in previous times men acted as hunters, whilst women were carers. This view also carries with it the assumption that since behaviour is natural, it cannot be fundamentally changed.

The debate over whether human beings or their societies are more influenced by nature or by learnt behaviour (eg culture), is termed the nature/nurture debate. Sociologists would argue that the concept of culture shows us that many aspects of our lives are not 'natural', but are ways of living that we have learnt. The study of people who have, for various reasons, missed out the vital stages of learning a culture, indicate that human behaviour is cultural behaviour.

Study point
• Suggest how the following aspects of behaviour could be influenced by social rules: eating, sexuality, aggression.

WHAT IS CULTURE?

In everyday use, the word culture is often used to refer to music, art and literature. Sociologists can use the term to refer to these activities, but they also use the concept in a wider sense. In fact different sociologists use the word 'culture' in rather different ways.

There are many definitions of culture, but it can be argued that there are two main definitions which are most important in sociology.

• A general definition comes from structural theories and defines culture as the 'way of life' of a society. This view assumes that there is a shared way of life within a society, with shared norms and values, which binds the society together.

- A more specific definition of culture comes from interpretivist theories, which see it as comprising the shared meanings and symbols which people use to convey meaning. The most obvious way in which members of a society share meanings is through using the same language. Groups of people with similar interests and outlook often develop their own language. Examples would be people in the same job, followers of particular types of music, people from the same social class or people from a particular area in a country or city. The slang and jargon which such groups use can serve to identify the members to each other and helps to reinforce their sense of identity. When we say that people will 'know what we mean' we are saying that meanings are shared.

Societies may also develop their own symbols such as badges, types of clothing, tattoos or perhaps jewellery, which will give particular coded messages to other members of the culture. For instance, in Britain married people wear a ring to signify their status and it is customary to wear black at funerals. We 'read' these symbols as signs which guide our behaviour in particular situations.

Study point

- Suggest some other examples of cultural symbols or signs, and show how they can guide behaviour.

There is some degree of similarity between both of these definitions of culture, since both focus upon shared understandings, but the first is a more structural view, whilst the second is associated with an interpretivist (or interactionist) approach, seeing meanings as being more open to interpretation.

Zygmunt Bauman points out that the word culture refers to something which is artificial, and therefore not natural. Bauman uses gardening as a metaphor for his view of culture. A garden is not natural; on the contrary, it is cultivated (a word with the same origin as culture), and plants are set out in a particular order or 'trained'. Bauman argues that, in a similar way, society trains individuals to follow a certain cultural code, which is indicated by signs such as clothes, symbols and words. Those who know the code know how to behave in particular circumstances, and therefore understand the meaning of the code, whether it is expressed through words or some other symbol, such as clothes.

According to Bauman cultural codes involve a system of opposing signs; so for instance, what counts as masculine behaviour is defined in contrast (or opposition) to feminine behaviour. The effect of this is to produce order and regularity in social life, which depends upon people acting in predictable ways if they are to be understood. If people break the code (or rules), then it is harder to understand the meaning of their actions. Culture thus becomes an artificial social order, which is continually being reproduced. Because it governs all our activity and behaviour, it is very hard to study, since it forms our taken for granted assumptions, and things which are really cultural aspects of behaviour are frequently seen as natural (eg gender differences). It is because of this Bauman says, that culture acts as a form of control. The concept of culture then, allows the sociologist to delve into the meaning and significance of social behaviour.

Bauman also points out that cultures, whether they be of a nation, a class, an ethnic group or some other social group, tend to be hostile to those outside the culture. This is because cultures intend to create order and uniformity, on the basis of a shared cultural code. Those who break the codes also break the rules, and become subject to sanctions which re-assert social uniformity.

THE ELEMENTS OF CULTURE — NORMS AND VALUES

We all learn the culture of our society by learning customs and habits. These customs and habits are referred to as norms by many sociologists. Norms are shared rules about behaviour. A society will have a variety of shared norms, such as working from Monday to Friday, celebrating Christmas Day, men retiring at 65 and so on. All these norms are part of our culture but in other societies life would be ordered differently. For instance not all societies have the same idea of work as that which is predominant in Britain and in these it may be that the idea of the 'weekend' simply does not exist.

Learning about the culture you have been born into means learning the rules about what is and is not acceptable behaviour in every area of society, such as education, the family and work. Sociologists call this process socialisation. The example of the weekend given above, indicates the way in which our culture involves socialisation into certain ideas about how long and when we should work. In all areas of life there will be rules which we are encouraged to follow. The various rules governing our behaviour can be seen as two distinct types, norms and values:

- Norms refer to common and agreed ways of behaviour in various social activities.
- Values are more general guidelines which indicate the social arrangements which we see as desirable and may be treated as goals to aim for.

Study point

- List four norms and values which are shared or agreed upon in British society. Consider to what extent norms and values are shared.

These various customs and habits in a society are the parts of its culture and together they form its cultural system. Also important to this view of culture are the objects that culture produces, the material goods, products, and the tools that people use in their everyday lives, eg cars, computers, books, clothes, tools. These objects are sometimes called 'material culture', and can be used to indicate status, or to make cultural or social statements. For instance, by wearing a piece of expensive jewellery, a T-shirt with a slogan, or by choosing to buy a particular type of car, people say something about the sort of person they are. People may be very conscious of what it is they are trying to say about themselves, or it may be something which they are only partly conscious of, but others will certainly judge an individual by making their own interpretations of such possessions. Thus the objects which we use in everyday life take on a symbolic meaning, and it is this which sociologists are interested in examining.

Activity

Conduct class research using examples from the media to demonstrate the symbolic use of material culture. Divide into groups and examine the following aspects of material culture: cars, clothes, and types of food.

SOCIALISATION AND SOCIAL CONTROL

Sociologists suggest that we learn the culture of our society through the process of socialisation. Socialisation refers to the way in which we absorb the rules of behaviour which are common in our society. Learning norms and values is a key part of the process of socialisation into a culture. Norms and values equip us to take up roles in society. Roles are simply the norms and values which are associated with particular positions in society. A man might have several roles, such as father, son, brother, husband, employee. In each of these social positions different norms of behaviour will be expected of the man. In different cultures the various roles referred to will vary, eg the role of a father – the expected behaviour for this role is different in Britain to that in say, China or Uganda.

Many sociologists would argue that norms, values and roles are not simply things which we can choose to follow if we like. They are all enforced by society through a system of sanctions. Sanctions are rewards or punishments, and society can usually force us to follow its rules by applying these. Sanctions may be formal, which means that they are considered important enough for there to be laws about them, or informal, which means that they are less important. In Britain it is a norm to get married and have children. Sanctions encourage us to do this, by providing various tax benefits to married couples with children, for instance. Cohabiting by contrast, is discouraged, and those who simply 'live together' may face legal problems as a consequence of their relationship. Informally, friends or relatives may feel a need to show disapproval of a couple who are cohabiting, and so may break off relations. However, it is also true that norms and values change over time, and cohabitation is now becoming much more common, and much more socially acceptable.

AGENCIES OF SOCIALISATION

The process of socialisation is conducted and controlled through social institutions, such as the family, the school, the Church, and the mass media. These are termed the agencies of socialisation (an agency is simply a mechanism, so the term refers to the mechanisms which enable socialisation to occur). These institutions play an important role in teaching and sanctioning desired norms and values. They are therefore very important cultural institutions.

The family socialises us into the norms and values of our culture in various ways. We learn for instance, about gender roles in the family. These can be some of our most formative influences, teaching us the roles our culture provides for men and women. This is not to say that these cultural norms and values are always upheld. Some men may find that the role of breadwinner is not one which they enjoy, and may become househusbands. Sexuality is now a common area of conflict with cultural norms as some people find that they prefer to express their sexuality through a gay relationship. In both of these examples, other institutions, such as schools, the Church and the mass media tend to reinforce the dominant cultural norms. All of these institutions will tend to encourage the conventional nuclear family and heterosexual marriage and there are various laws outlawing the marriage of gays and the promotion of homosexuality in schools. Since all these cultural institutions work together to uphold the same culture, sociologists talk of a cultural system.

Study point
• Suggest what might happen to a person who for some reason, misses the experience of socialisation.

PERSPECTIVES ON SOCIALISATION AND THE TRANSMISSION OF CULTURE

The various sociological perspectives see socialisation and the transmission of culture as occuring in several ways and as fulfilling various functions. A central issue which has to be considered is whether culture is to be seen as a structure or in terms of action, that is as something which human beings actively create through their own actions and decisions. This is the well known structure/action debate. Functionalists and Marxists, despite their differences, tend to see culture as something which is part of social structure, and which therefore forces (or determines) our behaviour in certain directions. Social action theories on the other hand, such as symbolic interactionism, tend to see culture as the result of a process of negotiation, and therefore as a reflection of human creativity. Human behaviour and culture seen in terms of the social action perspective is much less constrained (it is said to be voluntary or voluntaristic).

It is of course not necessary simply to take one side or the other on this debate. The sociologist **Anthony Giddens** has argued that the debate between structure and action approaches is best resolved by acknowledging that both are important in explaining social behaviour. Giddens suggests a synthesis is needed, and attempts to provide one through his theory of structuration. This argues that society is best understood as the result of both structure and action. Structures are created by peoples' actions, but they then influence the behaviour of others in turn. This argument can, of course, be directly applied to the topic of culture.

POSTMODERNISM AND SOCIALISATION

The view of socialisation and culture offered by the theories mentioned above, has recently been subjected to considerable criticism. Postmodernist theory has provided an alternative view, arguing that societies are no longer characterised by one dominant or shared culture. In postmodern societies there is, in contrast, a complex and diverse range of cultural norms and values, all coexisting, though not necessarily peacefully. In postmodern society, cultural norms and values are largely derived from the mass media. Thus postmodernists claim that individuals can adopt the norms and values of any particular group they aspire to – all they have to do is watch TV, decide which lifestyle they like, and then buy the relevant cultural symbols, such as clothes, car, music, books and so on.

Whereas structural theories tended to see individuals as trapped, or constrained, by their position in social structures, such as class, ethnicity or gender, postmodernists argue that such structures are of much less relevance in contemporary society. Socialisation and culture are much more flexible processes than modernist theories implied, and individuals are now able to 'pick and mix' cultural norms and values from a wide range of cultures on offer. Postmodernists conclude that culture is fragmenting. These theoretical differences have led some to emphasise a difference between postmodernist theories and modernist theories, which will be discussed in further detail elsewhere (see Chapter 9).

- Suggest evidence for the view that individuals can 'pick and mix' cultural values and cultural symbols.

PROBLEMS OF DEFINITION

Culture is a contested concept – it is defined in various ways. Several terms are used to try and distinguish between certain types or levels of culture. The main types of culture discussed in sociology are: High culture, Popular (or mass or low) culture and Folk culture.

HIGH CULTURE

Culture is often thought of as referring to the world of art, theatre, opera and classical music. It is exactly these areas which are considered to be 'high culture', both by sociologists and by the general public. This view of culture usually refers to the best artistic creations that a society has produced. Sociologists influenced by Marxist views would argue that the definition of high culture is determined by the economically dominant classes. It is their tastes which decide what counts as culture. Those who define culture as 'high culture' would probably argue that television, pop music and so-called 'pop art' should not be considered as being as good as, or on the same level as, theatre, classical music or classic paintings, for instance. The question arises though, as to who decides whether a piece of theatre, music or art is to be defined as being 'the best'.

For many sociologists the idea of high culture shows how the tastes of the economically dominant classes dominate the culture of a society. This is reflected not just in the arts, but throughout society, eg in education, where the study of the arts (high culture) remains extremely prestigious.

POPULAR CULTURE

High culture is often contrasted with popular culture. The term popular culture is generally used to refer to cultural activities which developed with the rise of industrial capitalism. Popular culture is often contrasted in a negative way with high culture, and may be portrayed as being shallow and meaningless. Popular culture in this sense refers to cultural activities or products which are popular – that is , are enjoyed by very large numbers of people. Some may use the term low culture to refer to popular culture, which reinforces the idea that the activities and products referred to are of less worth than 'high culture' activities or products. Others might use the term 'mass culture', indicating those cultural products which are produced and distributed using mass production technology. For many sociologists making a distinction between high and popular culture serves to identify activities in terms of high and low status, and generally reflects class differences.

FOLK CULTURE

The distinction between high and popular culture is one which has developed with the rise of industrial capitalism. Folk culture refers to the cultural activities and art forms of the 'ordinary' people in pre-industrial or rural societies, eg folk dancing, folk art and music, customs and traditions (folklore). It can still be of relevance in societies which have not industrialised, or have done so fairly recently.

The idea of folk culture lives on today in our concepts of 'folk music' and in elements of New Age culture, which identifies with a 'back to nature' point of view. Marxists may take the view that folk culture was a more authentic form of culture, which the process of industrialisation has destroyed and replaced with an artificial and mass produced popular culture which merely has the effect of drugging people into acceptance of capitalist society. For those who see culture in terms of high culture, folk culture may be regarded as being rather crude and primitive.

For sociologists the existence of different levels of culture raises interesting sociological questions about which social groups have the power successfully to define behaviour or activities as high, popular or folk culture, whether there is consensus about these categories and judgements, and about the role and functions that the categories play in society.

Activity

Suggest examples of cultural activities and products representing each level of culture, eg high culture – opera, visiting art galleries. Devise a semi-structured interview to elicit the cultural preferences of members of different social classes.

WHAT IS IDENTITY?

It has been a common view that sociology has little to say about personality and individual identity, these traditionally being seen as more appropriately left to psychology. The views of human nature predominant in industrialised societies often suggest that personality is something fixed and innate, and this has been reflected in some schools of psychological and sociological thought.

- Structuralist sociologists however, whilst not wishing to suggest that there are no aspects of our personality which can be explained in terms of either genetic structure, or biochemistry or physiology, argue that our sense of identity is largely the product of social factors.

- Interactionists would argue that the very sense of being an individual, and the way in which we are encouraged to perceive ourselves as individuals, is socially constructed. It is our culture which leads us to think of ourselves first and foremost as individuals, rather than as family members. Moreover, in modern society, culture has tended to lead us to think of ourselves in particular terms; identity has mainly been conceived of, so modernist theories claim, in terms of class, ethnicity or gender. The link between identity and culture can be seen to be a very close one indeed.

- **Bauman** argues that identity is created in opposition to other identities, which themselves are set by the cultural code. For example, the range of identities open for a middle class person, involve defining themselves partly in terms of some category which they are different to, in this case an upper class or a working class person.

- Postmodernists have been highly critical of modernist theories which have appeared to narrow the key constituents of personal identity down to class, ethnicity and gender. Such a focus leads to a very impoverished and narrow view of social reality. On the contrary, many individuals refuse to be pigeon-holed by these social categories.

- Sociologists need to be sensitive to differences within class, ethnic and gender groups. There may be just as important differences within the working class as between the working and the middle class, and between women from different social groups, and so on.

- In trying to be scientific, over-ambitious modernist theories have fallen into the mistake of believing their own claims of objectivity, and this has led them to over-generalise and to neglect differences within key social groups. Just as postmodernists claim that culture in contemporary society is fragmenting, so too, they suggest, is our notion of individual identity.

- It is harder for individuals to define themselves adequately in contemporary society, since there is such a range of competing sources of identity. The old sources of identity, such as class, ethnicity and gender, are no longer uniform and cohesive entities. This makes contemporary society a very different environment for individuals to live in than modern society, and it leads to different types of individual, different types of living, and different types of social groups, structures and processes. Postmodernists argue that contemporary society is undergoing dramatic social change; if sociology is to adequately understand that change, it has to change some of its way of thinking.

SUMMARY

Sociologists disagree about how to define culture and about the role it plays in society, and it is therefore a contested concept. Mainly as a result of theoretical debates within sociology, culture and identity are now central topics of discussion.

However, it can be agreed that, despite the range of debate, much human behaviour is best understood as cultural, or learnt behaviour, rather than simply as 'natural', or as the result of biological factors. This is not, however, to deny that there are no aspects of human behaviour which are caused by biological factors, but rather to point out that these are only part, not the whole explanation. Studying culture is a difficult task, since it requires sociologists to attempt to shed the influences of their own culture, learnt over a lifetime, and critically to examine their most basic assumptions.

The following three chapters examine the place of the concepts of culture and identity in mainstream sociological theory, before going on to examine them in the context of the key topic areas of class, gender and ethnicity. The final chapter returns to current debates about contemporary culture, identity and society.

STUDY GUIDES

Group Work

1 Examine a selection of fashion, youth culture, or lifestyle magazines. Discuss how they may influence the process of socialisation, and the effects they may have on identity.

2 Hold discussions to consider how successful the process of socialisation is. Try to provide examples which show the extent to which norms and values are either broken or adhered to, and the various sanctions which may apply. Consider how these observations affect your evaluation of the concept of socialisation.

3 Conduct a class debate on the nature/nurture debate. Prepare thoroughly by researching into cases of unsocialised individuals. Try to include examples from books on other subjects, eg genetics, physiology, psychology. Issues for discussion may include gender differences, intelligence differences, and ethnic differences.

Practice Questions

ITEM A

Ralph Linton states that "The culture of a society is the way of life of its members; the collection of ideas and habits which they learn, share and transmit from generation to generation". In Clyde Kluckhohn's elegant phrase, culture is a "design for living" held by members of a particular society. Since humans have no instincts to direct their actions, their behaviour must be based on guidelines which are learned. In order for a society to operate effectively, these guidelines must be shared by its members. Without a shared culture, members of society would be unable to communicate and cooperate, and confusion and disorder would result. Culture therefore has two essential qualities: firstly it is learned, secondly it is shared. Without it there would be no human society.

Haralambos and Holborn, Sociology Themes and Perspectives, Harper Collins, 1990, p5

ITEM B

There were always numerous problems with Dowayo 'explanations'. Firstly they missed out the essential piece of information that made things comprehensible. No one told me that this village was where the Master of the Earth, the man who controlled the fertility of all plants, lived, and that consequently various parts of the ceremony would be different from elsewhere. This is fair enough; some things are too obvious to mention. If we were explaining to a Dowayo how to drive a car, we should tell him all sorts of things about gears and road signs before mentioning that one tried not to hit other cars.

Nigel Barley, The Innocent Anthropologist, Penguin, 1983, p82

1 What criticism of the sociobiological perspective is made in Item A?   (2)
2 With reference to the Items and elsewhere, explain how individuals are socialised into a culture.   (5)
3 Using material from elsewhere, explain the sociological significance of studies of unsocialised individuals.   (5)
4 With reference to Item B and elsewhere, explain why culture is a difficult topic for sociologists to study.   (5)
5 With reference to the Items and elsewhere, evaluate the view that human behaviour is largely cultural.   (8)

Coursework

1 Conduct an investigation into the process of socialisation, focusing upon a particular social category, such as gender, class, ethnicity or age.
2 Produce an ethnography of a social group. You could make an indepth study of a particular occupational group, a youth culture, or a group of friends with a shared leisure interest, eg a football team. What are the norms and values of the group, and what insights do they give to the behaviour and culture of group members?
3 Conduct a critical investigation into sociobiological theories of human behaviour. Examine whether such theories can be usefully applied to areas such as sexuality or health.

3

THE FUNCTIONALIST APPROACH TO CULTURE AND IDENTITY

Introduction

FUNCTIONALISM IS A modernist theory of society. Functionalists such as Durkheim saw industrialisation as leading to social structures which differed in profound ways from those of traditional societies. Industrialisation and a specialised division of labour, where an individual would have one highly specialised job rather than being involved in the whole production process, led to a society with very different social relationships. There was also a move away from the countryside and towns and cities began to develop rapidly. This in turn meant the decline of tightly knit communities, where it was possible, for example, for an individual to know the names of most of the people living in their village. It also saw an expansion of opportunities for work. No longer was it necessary to stay in the same place and to take up the same work as your parents, or to be offered apprenticeship to a limited number of trades for those who could afford it. Industrialisation saw the birth of mass society. Mass society however, brought problems with it.

- Large numbers of people living in close proximity necessitated organisational changes in society, especially given the specialised division of labour which was developing.
- It was no longer possible to rely upon friends and family to provide care for the sick and elderly, to provide education, or even to provide work.
- Whilst mass society offered many opportunities and the chance to escape from the constraints of traditional society, it also involved individuals having to accept greater risk and uncertainty in their lives and lifechances.

This chapter examines how functionalist theory defines and explains the role of culture and how it affects identity in industrial society.

Table 2: *Theorists, concepts and issues in this chapter*

KEY THEORISTS	KEY CONCEPTS	KEY ISSUES
• Emile Durkheim	Differentiation	What is the difference between traditional society and modern industrial society?
• Talcott Parsons	Structural differentiation	
• Robert Merton	Integration	What are the functions of culture?
• Dennis Wrong	Value consensus	How does modern industrial society affect individual identity?
	Anomie	
	Industrial society	How useful is the functionalist view in explaining the role and nature of culture and identity in modern society?
	Subcultures	

FUNCTIONALISM, SOCIETY AND THE INDIVIDUAL

Emile Durkheim is generally seen as one of the founders of modern sociology, and one of the first functionalists. Durkheim's work provides an important analysis of the nature of culture and identity in modern industrial societies, challenging sociobiological (see chapter 2), and individualistic theories of human behaviour.

Durkheim argued that it was erroneous to attempt to explain social events in terms of the behaviour or characteristics of individuals. For example, it would be misleading to try and explain crime as being simply the behaviour of innately bad people, or suicide as being the action of innately disturbed people. Durkheim argued that in fact these types of events had social causes – that is larger social forces affect individuals lives. Moreover, Durkheim argued that even our individual sense of identity is the result of being socialised into a modern society.

DURKHEIM – CULTURE, IDENTITY AND MORAL ORDER

These ideas are discussed in detail in two of Durkheim's key sociological studies – *The Division of Labour in Society*, and *Suicide*. In *The Division of Labour in Society*, Durkheim put forward the idea that the transition from traditional to industrial society, in changing the way work is organised, has important social consequences. Durkheim was interested in the way in which societies were integrated – the way they work as whole societies, rather than just as collections of individuals. Durkheim suggested that traditional society could best be seen as working in terms of what he called mechanical solidarity. Traditional society was integrated, or held together, by the fact that people had similar beliefs and values and the roles available in society were basically the same. Thus in traditional village life in pre-industrial society, whilst there would be some specialisation, all would live a similar life, perhaps doing a little farming, and a variety of other types of work. Traditional society can be seen as being rather like Britain in the early industrial revolution, with smallholders combining small scale farming with weaving, and perhaps other workers, such as small shopkeepers or traders, also doing some small scale farming. Identities were clearly defined in terms of role and family background.

Industrialisation in contrast, saw the transition to a society based upon organic solidarity. With the specialisation of roles demanded by industrial production, people moved to towns and cities. Functionalists talk of the separation of home and work. Work was no longer something which occurred at home and which could be controlled by the individual. Manufacturers wanted large scale production and this demanded that workers and the work process were placed in specialised accommodation. With specialised roles came what functionalists term functional differentiation – the creation of many different and specialised occupational roles, although it was not just these sorts of roles which were affected as will be seen. Identity became a more complex issue as people experienced more dimensions to their lives.

The modern individual, for Durkheim, was created by industrialisation and the resultant division of labour based upon organic solidarity. All of this however, was based upon a social consensus – an agreed moral order. Durkheim assumed that societies were ultimately held together, or integrated, by shared values (moral order). One of the problems of the transition to industrial society was that shared values were thrown into doubt in a period of rapid social change. People became more confused as to their identities and their roles. Durkheim argued that this was indeed the case throughout the industrial revolution and the nineteenth century, with high rates of socially disruptive behaviour such as divorce, crime, strikes and suicide. Durkheim termed such a situation as 'anomic'. The concept of anomie refers to a lack of controlling norms. Durkheim felt that modern industrial societies would over-emphasise the importance of individuality, and that this would erode social stability and solidarity.

- Provide examples of the ways in which modern societies reflect a focus upon the individual.

SUICIDE, IDENTITY AND SOCIAL INTEGRATION

Durkheim's view of the socially constructed nature of the individual is perhaps best illustrated by his study of suicide. Durkheim argued that suicide, apparently the most individual act it is possible to imagine, was directly related to the degree of social integration a person experienced in a society. Durkheim argued that social integration itself was adequately indicated by religious affiliation, and he argued that Catholicism reflected a tight knit and highly solidaristic society, whereas Protestant communities were less socially integrated. Thus Durkheim was able to hypothesise that high social integration (Catholic identity) would lead to a lower suicide rate, whilst low social integration (Protestant identity) would lead to higher suicide rates. The underlying argument here was that where individuals were situated in highly integrated societies, there would be more pressure or support, preventing individuals from committing or wanting to commit suicide. By contrast, in societies characterised by low social integration, with weak solidarity and shared norms, anomic suicide would be much more likely.

POINTS OF EVALUATION

Durkheim's studies indicate that modern industrial society created a particular sort of identity, which differed greatly from the identity available to those living in traditional societies. They also demonstrate that even our own self identity is something which is socially constructed, and which varies depending upon the sort of society which we happen to live in. It is now appropriate to examine how modern societies create differences between individuals and between different sectors within society.

Study point

- Suggest ways in which, according to Durkheim, individuals in modern society would be different to individuals in traditional society.

MODERNITY AND DIFFERENTIATION

A key insight provided by functionalism has been to stress the way in which modern society differentiates us as individuals – in freeing us from the ties of a traditional society, industrialisation makes us different from each other. The American functionalist **Talcott Parsons** argues that this occurs as a result of the process of structural differentiation.

By the term structural differentiation, Parsons refers to the way in which industrialisation led to an increasingly complex system of institutions in the industrialising societies. As a functionalist, Parsons would agree that all societies have certain essential needs, functional prerequisites, such as a need for food (economics, production), shelter, clothing and some way of organising society (politics). In simple societies, such as tribes of hunter-gatherers these can all be achieved with very simple organisational structures. The need for education for example, can be met fairly simply, perhaps by parents and elders teaching children necessary skills for hunting. Pre-industrial society was clearly not so simple, but it was still possible for societies to function with a rudimentary organisational structure. In terms of work for instance, technology and the scale of production meant that the division of labour – the range of skills and jobs available – was fairly limited.

The coming of industrialisation, however, meant that the task of meeting the needs of society became much more complex. An expanding and increasingly complex division of labour led to a requirement for a much wider range of skills in the labour force. This in turn affected all aspects of life, such as education, the family, and political institutions. Equally, changes in political and social institutions had effects on economic organisation.

CULTURE AND IDENTITY IN MODERN SOCIETY –
FROM ASCRIPTION TO ACHIEVEMENT

As society industrialised it became much more complex, so the roles available to individuals changed. Roles in traditional society can be seen as having been relatively fixed and stable, and to a considerable degree fixed at birth. Parsons describes traditional society as being based on ascription – an individual's role and status is ascribed or given at birth and is inherited from parents. Thus the child born into an aristocratic family would be destined for a very different future from a child whose father was a farm labourer, regardless of individual merit. In modern society however, roles are achieved, and are the result of individual ability and effort. Parsons thus sees modern industrial society as being meritocratic – the position and role which individuals achieve reflects their ability, and is not fixed at birth as it is in traditional society.

MULTIPLE ROLES

Parsons analysis emphasises that in contrast to traditional society, where individuals would be largely tied to one role, industrial society is so complex that individuals have to be seen as having several roles, with complex implications for identity. In traditional society, since most work was conducted at home, occupational roles were fused with family roles. In modern society home and work are usually separated, with individuals working and living in separate places. Thus individuals in modern society can have a variety of roles and identities.

For functionalists such a situation can lead to role conflict, a situation where the demands of different roles conflict with each other. This leads to situations whereby the behaviour expected from a person differs from that which one has been led to expect, causing confusion. An example would be the case of working mothers. Social values generally expect women to take the affective (caring) role, and to be based in the home looking after a family. Functionalists argue that society only works because of the existence of shared norms and values. Thus it is assumed that women's role is to be the carer and homemaker. Members of society learn that this is a norm and accordingly are able to organise their lives around a stable set of assumptions and rules. However, as more women are now taking on careers as well as being wives and mothers, their roles are changing, thus causing role conflict. As a result there may be an increase in divorce as women and men have differing views as to which role is appropriate for each other.

Functionalism demonstrates that modern society has created a particular type of individual, stressing the different roles available to us. Roles are not simply the result of natural differences between individuals, but are the result of socialisation into particular norms and values. Norms and values in turn are to be seen as part of the culture of a society. Culture plays a key role in functionalism, and it is this which must now be examined.

Activity

Conduct a survey of married women who combine a career with being a housewife. Investigate whether there is any experience of role conflict, and the extent to which the women hold shared norms and values. If possible, it may be interesting to compare women's views with those of men. Are there shared cultural assumptions about women's role and identity in our society?

Study point

- To what extent do you agree that roles in modern society are achieved? Are there no aspects of ascription left in modern society?

FUNCTIONALISM AND CULTURE

Functionalist sociologists such as Durkheim and Parsons saw culture as being of vital importance in integrating societies. Without shared norms and values, they argued, societies would disintegrate into anarchy and chaos. Culture could therefore be seen as a sort of 'social glue', holding the various parts of society together and enabling them to function effectively.

Talcott Parsons is particularly important in this context, since he was most concerned to see how culture contributed to social stability, and culture therefore plays a central role in his version of functionalism. The central assumption in Parsons' theory was that societies had four key needs, or functional prerequisites. Parsons refers to the needs of goal attainment, adaptation, integration and pattern maintenance.

Goal attainment
- By goal attainment, Parsons referred to the need for societies to set goals or aims, such as for instance, economic growth, eliminating poverty, or perhaps, being the most powerful nation on earth.

Adaptation
- Adaptation refers to the need societies have to adapt to their environment, with particular reference to the natural resources for life which may or may not be available in any particular geographical location. Societies based in a very rich environment will clearly be different and adapt in different ways compared to societies based in arid desert conditions.

Integration
- Integration refers to the need a society will have to manage conflicts in some way. This mainly refers to internal conflicts between members of the society.

Pattern maintenance
- Pattern maintenance refers to the need to maintain the basic pattern of shared values.

However, for Parsons, individual behaviour or action has to be seen as occurring in the context of social institutions. Institutions themselves are the result of the functional prerequisites and inevitably bring about the development of specialising systems to fulfil and organise necessary functions. Central to this though is the role of the cultural system which helps integrate society; its key role is in bringing about social change. Human behaviour and identity then, has to be seen as institutionalised – it is something which we are socialised into, and it is through this process that we acquire status and roles. This view has been one of the dominant versions of functionalism. However, some sociologists have been sceptical of the idea that socialisation into shared norms and values is always so successful, and they have argued that Parsons' theory does not seem to allow for the existence of subcultures.

FUNCTIONALISM AND SUBCULTURES

The American sociologist **Robert Merton** was the first functionalist to challenge the idea that societies were characterised by a common culture. Unusually for a functionalist, Merton argued that in an unequal society, individuals would not have an equal chance of achieving the goals identified by the common culture. Merton thought that this would lead individuals to abandon the socially acceptable routes to achieving cultural goals, or even in some cases, abandon the goals themselves. Merton therefore devised his own typology (classification) of responses to cultural goals – Conformity, Innovation, Ritualism, Retreatism, and Rebellion. Merton thus argued that individuals would respond to the cultural goals of society in different ways.

Conformity

- Conformists would support the goals of society, even if they felt that the means of achieving the goal was not available to them.

Innovation

- Merton gives the name 'innovator' to those individuals who, whilst supporting the common goals of society, find that the means of achieving these is not available to them. According to this typology for example, the child who is unsuccessful in school becomes the classroom clown in order to achieve status.

Ritualism

- Merton sees those who have ceased to aspire to some of the goals of society despite having the means to compete, and yet still adhere to the rules, as ritualists. Their lives consist in a dull and monotonous conformity to goals which they no longer feel any enthusiasm for. They are simply 'going through the motions' and have no real commitment to social goals. They give up any ambitions they may have had to chase social goals, and are too scared to break the rules – the result of very successful socialisation into shared norms and values.

Retreatism

- Retreatists are those who reject both the goals and the accepted means of achieving goals, and become drop-outs. The category could thus be applied to a diverse range of people, such as tramps, drug addicts, new age travellers and people living in communes.

Rebellion

- Rebels go a stage further than retreatists. They are not content simply to reject social goals and the usual means of achieving them, but want to replace them with alternative goals and alternative institutional structures by which to achieve such goals. Examples, here could include revolutionary groups and terrorist groups, and even some religious cults.

Study point
- Suggest examples for each of Merton's categories.

Merton's modification of functionalist theory is a valuable one. Merton's theory is sometimes referred to as a 'strain theory', since it highlights the fact that there may be tension between the cultural goals of a society, and the institutionalised means to achieving such goals. Merton does not insist on the idea that certain institutions are essential and inevitable, arguing instead that functional prerequisites may be met in a variety of different ways. Merton provides a more flexible interpretation of functionalism and argues that it is possible to think in terms of the degree of functionality and balance achieved by a social system.

POINTS OF EVALUATION

One prominent criticism is that Merton deals only with individual responses to the cultural system. In contrast to Parsons, Merton sees criminal behaviour as deviant, or abnormal, and as something which is solely an individual response. Other sociologists such as **Albert Cohen**, **Cloward** and **Ohlin**, and **Walter Miller**, have seen criminal behaviour not as an individual response to a particular social environment, but as a shared collective response. Thus these latter authors are able to introduce the concept of a subculture.

SUBCULTURAL THEORIES

A subculture can be seen as a distinctive set of cultural values which whilst sharing some aspects of a common culture, also differ in some important ways. Cohen for instance, believes that it is possible to think of criminal subcultures as distinct adaptations to particular social contexts, where the main cultural values are replaced by alternative norms and values. Cohen illustrates this by the example of crimes without purpose, pointing out that Merton's discussion of crime assumed that crime had to have a purpose. As Cohen notes, this is not true of all crime, such as joy-riding, or gratuitous violence. Cohen argues that such crimes arise out of status frustration, not simply need. Those who are denied the ability to participate fully in society, thus take out their frustration by devising alternative systems of values and norms, which do provide them with the means of gaining status and self-esteem. These are however, collective endeavours, being characteristic of whole neighbourhoods, not simply odd individuals.

The idea of 'honour among thieves' could be seen as illustrating the differences and similarities between a criminal subculture and the common culture of the wider society. Criminal subcultures develop their own norms and values, which may for instance portray the act of stealing from shops, as being 'fair game'. The criminal subculture, however, may see stealing from other members of the criminal community as being dishonest. Another interesting example could be the well known 'criminal' dislike of sex offenders. Here the 'criminal' subculture shares some common values with the wider society. Nevertheless, in other significant ways, criminal groups can be seen to develop a distinct set of norms and values, which can be seen as a subculture, a variant of the common culture.

Activity
Conduct a questionnaire to examine the norms and values of young people. Do young people generally share the norms and values of the wider (older) population, or are they radically different? Compare your results with research findings from Social Trends or a recent British Social Attitudes Survey.

CRITICISMS OF FUNCTIONALISM

Functionalism is very much a modernist theory of society. It offers a 'grand theory' to explain everything in society, and it espouses a belief that sociology can be a science of society by using empirical and frequently quantitative research methods, which can then contribute to and inform the social policy-making process. In relation to culture and identity several main criticisms can be made of functionalist theories.

1   Functionalism tends to neglect conflict. Inevitably, by focusing on the concept of shared norms and values, and value consensus, functionalists run the risk of exaggerating the degree to which there actually are shared values. Culture does not always act as an integrating 'social glue', as the many conflicts over cultural differences demonstrate. Examining the various definitions of culture – a way of life, artistic activity or symbolic systems of meaning – demonstrates that there is considerable disagreement on cultural issues.

2   Functionalism presents us with a view of human beings which some have argued is 'oversocialised'. All behaviour appears to be learnt and socialisation appears to be an inevitable process which rarely if ever fails. As **Dennis Wrong**

has argued, it is important to recognise that human beings are also part of the natural world, and are not immune from some natural processes. Many sociologists draw upon the work of the psychologist **Sigmund Freud** to illustrate the view that understanding human behaviour must acknowledge some role for nature in explaining human identity and culture.

3 Many sociologists are critical of the deterministic aspects of functionalism. Functionalism is a structural theory, and by seeing culture as a part of the structure of society, functionalism can make it seem inevitable that individuals will adopt the cultural norms and values of society. Many sociologists influenced by interactionist theories would argue that as reflexive (thinking) beings, people have more freedom to make choices and decisions than functionalism assumes.

POINTS OF EVALUATION

Despite its weaknesses, functionalist views of culture do have some merits. In contrast to sociobiological views, functionalism does stress that culture is an aspect of social structure and is socially constructed. Related to this is the recognition in functionalist thought that culture is learnt and transmitted through the process of socialisation. Thus it could be argued that whatever its weaknesses it provides, at the very least, a starting point for a sociological analysis of culture and identity.

SUMMARY

Functionalism provides a rigorous theoretical attempt to explain the differences between traditional society and modern society, focusing on a structural approach to society. As has been indicated, not all sociologists would agree with some of the central assumptions of functionalist theory. Functionalists have tended to see culture in terms of the way of life of a society, and as reflecting the shared values which integrate a complex modern society. Another theoretical perspective, Marxism, whilst also taking a structural view of culture, has suggested that the concept of culture can be interpreted in a very different way. This is the subject of the next chapter.

Group Work

1 Conduct a class debate on the motion 'Britain has a common culture'.

2 Three groups should conduct research into the work of one of the following sociologists; Merton, Parsons or Durkheim, as well as generating a list of about five questions about the work of the other two sociologists. One member from each group will take the role of the key sociologist investigated and answer questions about his work from the rest of the class. Each key sociologist will take a turn to be interviewed in this way.

3 Create an evaluation chart (see introduction) of functionalist theories of culture and identity. Individually write a brief summary evaluation of the functionalist approach to culture and identity. If you have achieved a variety of opinion in the class, get one person who broadly favours the functionalist approach, and one who takes a pessimistic view of it, to read out their respective summaries.

Practice Questions

ITEM A: WHO DARES WRITES

Bravo Two Zero immerses the reader in a male subculture, offering the attractions of anthropology without the academic drawbacks. Reading *Bravo Two Zero* thus becomes a similar experience to watching a Disappearing World documentary about a warrior tribe such as the Masai or the Nuba. The SAS boasts its own village (the Hereford barracks), its own initiation ritual (the gruelling selection process of marches on the Brecon Beacons), its ancestors and heroes, its legendary events, its costume (informal by army standards), its magical symbols, its codes and taboos, and its unique style of mourning (auctioning off the dead man's kit). Plus, of course, its vision of women's role in the tribe: staying at home in Hereford having babies.

Teach Yourself SAS

'the Regiment' = 22 SAS, 'tab'= march, 'slot' = shoot dead, 'rupert' = officer, 'scaley' = signaller, 'slime' = intelligence corps, 'jundie' = Iraqi soldier, 'Bergen' = backpack, 'basha' = shelter, 'cuds' = the country, 'brew' = tea, 'scoff' = food, 'gob off' = speak, 'brick' = four man patrol, 'bone' = naff/stupid, 'Eppie Scoppie' = tantrum, 'go pear-shaped' = lose rag, 'on my chinstrap' = knackered, 'Head Shed' = high command/HQ, 'RTU'd' = returned to unit/fired, 'LUP' = lying up point, 'ERV' = emergency rendezvous, 'OC' = officer commanding, 'remf' = loser (rear-echelon motherfucker).

John Dugdale, The Guardian, 26.4.96

ITEM B

Durkheim's work can be usefully applied to gain an insight into the way in which the American educational system promotes a national culture. All American schools start the day with the oath of allegiance to the American flag, which is present in all classrooms. The American motto 'E Pluribus Unum' (out of many, one), reinforces the view that American society is a 'melting pot' where anyone, regardless of race, creed or class, can become an American citizen. The American education system can thus be seen as attempting to socialise students with a diverse range of cultural beliefs and practices into the American way of life.

David Abbott

1 Using examples from Item A, describe briefly the two senses in which sociologists define culture. (4)
2 Using Items A and B, identify three examples of cultural symbols. (3)
3 Item B suggests that the American education system aims to integrate students into a shared culture. Suggest three forms of social difference which might hamper such a project. (3)
4 Explain and evaluate the functionalist explanation of subcultures. (7)
5 Using evidence from the Items and elsewhere, evaluate the view that the function of culture is to integrate individuals into the shared norms and values of society. (8)

Coursework

1 Investigate the functionalist view of roles and identity. Are roles and identity in contemporary society ascribed or achieved? Examples worth considering might be gender roles or conjugal roles, or ethnic identity between different generations.
2 Conduct research to investigate how people cope with multiple roles and role conflict.
3 Apply subcultural theory to the study of an educational institution. What subcultures exist and what functions do they appear to have? To what extent do the subcultures share similar values to the wider society?

4

CULTURE, IDENTITY AND CAPITALISM

Introduction

MARXISM, LIKE FUNCTIONALISM, is another structural theory which aimed to provide a total theory of society, and which insisted that society could only be understood if seen as a whole. Apart from this common starting point however, the two theories have little in common, proceeding to develop very different explanations of modern society. Marxist concepts are flexible and adaptable and can be usefully interpreted and applied to questions about culture and identity. Furthermore, Marxism, in common with other theoretical traditions, is a body of theory which is continually being developed by successive generations of sociologists. Thus later Marxists, such as the members of the so-called Frankfurt School, and the Italian Marxist Antonio Gramsci, have focused a great deal more attention on cultural processes.

Like functionalists, Marxists agree that society is best understood as a system or as a structure. Marxists however, see modern societies as being class-based societies, consisting of two classes whose interests inevitably clash, resulting in endemic conflict. For Marxists, functionalists neglect one of the most important features of modern society. Modern societies are not simply industrial societies, they are also (mostly) capitalist societies. The term industrial implies mass production and the technology which makes it possible. Marxists wish to insist that it is of crucial significance to recognise that most industrial societies are also capitalist societies, meaning that the economic system aims to maximise profit, and assumes that society will be divided into two classes; owners and workers. This clearly has implications for the ways in which culture and identity can be defined and explained in such societies, and this chapter will examine the various ways in which Marxist theory conceptualises culture and identity.

Table 3: *Theorists, concepts and issues in this chapter*		
KEY THEORISTS	KEY CONCEPTS	KEY ISSUES
• Karl Marx • Louis Althusser • The Frankfurt School • Antonio Gramsci	Base-superstructure model Alienation Capitalism Commodity fetishism Ideology Mass culture	What is the role of culture and the nature of identity in capitalist society? How does the existence of class conflict in capitalist society influence culture and identity? How adequate are Marxist analyses of culture and identity?

TRADITIONAL SOCIETY AND CAPITALIST SOCIETY

While functionalists tend to see the transformation from traditional to industrial society as freeing people from the constraints of tradition and bringing about a society based upon meritocracy, Marxists have been much more pessimistic. For Marx, industrial society was also capitalist society and the freedoms it offered were 'formal'. Workers in capitalist societies, Marx pointed out, could indeed take their labour to the capitalist of their choice, a marked change from the serfdom of the medieval peasantry. However, for Marx this freedom was more apparent than real, since the worker was certainly not free from the constraints of capitalism – in other words the necessity to work and the resulting exploitation, poverty and inequality.

The Marxist base-superstructure model thus makes several key points about capitalist society:

- In capitalist societies production is organised to maximise profits for capitalists, not to fulfil the needs of society.
- The class structure consists of two classes, bourgeoisie and proletariat, or owners and workers.
- Individual identity is judged not on the grounds of an individual's achievements (as functionalists argue), but on the basis of the individual's class position.
- People are dehumanised, becoming seen as workers or employers, not as people.

Thus, for Marxists, the range of identities open to individuals in capital societies is severely constrained by their position in the class structure. Class position and the need to work become the central aspects of identity in capital societies. In a similar way, culture, rather than reflecting shared norms and values, is seen by

Marxists as reflecting the interests of the economically dominant classes. To explain why Marxists see culture in this way, it is necessary briefly to examine how Marxists conceptualise society.

Study point

- Suggest ways in which a person's class position could influence their sense of identity.

BASE-SUPERSTRUCTURE – THE MARXIST MODEL OF SOCIETY

Marxists see society as a structure or system, with interrelated parts. Whilst both Marxists and functionalists see society as a system, they have radically different views as to how such a system functions.

For Marxists, capitalist societies consist of two parts, base and superstructure. The base (or infrastructure) is essentially the economic system of society, and refers to the way a society meets its most essential needs, for food and shelter. Thus, in late nineteenth century Britain the economic base of society was organised on the basis of factory technology and mass production, whereas in late fifteenth century Britain the base was an agrarian economy, with agriculture being the dominant means of making a living for most of the population. The term 'means of production' is often used by Marxists to refer to the type of technology which is used to produce goods, eg in hunter-gatherer societies the means of production would be bows and arrows, whilst in more modern times industrial technology is the means of production.

The other major part of society is the superstructure. This consists of all the other parts of society, eg political, legal, educational and cultural systems, family structure, and so on. Marx argued that the superstructure always reflects the economic base of society, so that the type of economic production used by a society will determine the superstructure of that society. So in a hunter-gatherer society for example, political structures, reflecting the simplicity of the economic base and size of the society, will probably involve a council of the eldest members of the tribe. In a large scale industrial capitalist society, more complex institutional structures will develop.

Political institutions in industrial capitalist societies will reflect the class divisions within that society, and indeed will act as institutional channels for class conflict. In the hunter-gatherer society by contrast, there will be no classes, and no class conflict, since all will own the means of production (bows and arrows), and thus political institutions may be formed on the basis of some other factor, such as knowledge and experience of hunting. Nevertheless, the model still applies, since it is the economic base, and the means of production, which determine the superstructure of society. Thus, according to the Marxist model, the means of production of a society – the economy – determines the relations of production. This model is known as the base-superstructure model.

Marxism suggests that capitalist societies tend to produce a certain type of identity, one defined predominantly in terms of the relations of production, or in other words, in terms of class. Modern capitalism, far from being the land of opportunity, is seen as producing human beings who are stunted and deformed, or to use the phrase of **Herbert Marcuse**, 'one-dimensional man'. The concepts underlying this assessment must now be examined.

Study point

- Suggest how the national identity of a society could be influenced by the economy.

ALIENATION, COMMODITY FETISHISM AND IDENTITY

According to Marx, human nature was adaptable and largely shaped by environmental factors, the result of nurture rather than nature. Marx argued that people were social and creative beings. Human beings would thrive in the company of others, and by working together to make a living.

Marx suggests that there was a time in history, prior to the invention of private property, when such a state of affairs actually existed, (though the historical evidence for this must remain dubious). In such a period, Marx suggests that humans would be able to lead a fulfilled life, since they would be able to act according to their nature. However Marx argues that once private property was developed, a process he termed alienation begins, and reaches its height with the onset of industrial capitalism.

Alienation is a complex concept, but it can be simply described as meaning a state where human beings become separated from their true nature (or species-being). Marx argues that:

- Alienation starts with the invention of private property.
- Once private property is invented, a person's work is no longer their own – someone else, an employer, will take away the product of work and sell it for a profit.
- In capitalist societies social relationships between people become reduced to market relationships.
- In such a society people are defined in terms of how much money they earn,

whether they work, or the sort of work they do, and not in terms of human qualities.

- Capitalism creates false needs, which seduce the working classes into accepting capitalism. Thus for example, capitalism creates ever more attractive consumer goods which workers can enjoy in their leisure time.
- New technology has been developed not because we need it, but because it produces a profit for capitalists.
- This development of false needs leads to what is termed commodity fetishism. This simply means that in capitalist societies, people develop insatiable appetites for more and more new goods. This, for Marxists, is part and parcel of alienation for we cannot achieve true satisfaction or happiness in capitalist society.

Capitalism then, produces a culture which promotes the development of identities which are distortions of our true nature. It turns people into alienated workers and reduces human relationships to market relationships. Human beings come to be seen primarily as commodities, as labour power for instance. In this way, Marxists argue that a person's sense of personal worth and their role in society is shaped by their place in the social structure. They may develop a low status identity because they fail in school, gain few qualifications, and lead highly alienated lifestyles. The reverse may be true of those closer to positions of power and authority. Marxists produce a pessimistic view of modern society, with an equally pessimistic account of culture and identity in capitalist society. It is now necessary to consider the implications of this account for a Marxist view of culture and its role in society.

CULTURE AS IDEOLOGY

For the Marxist, it is not the case that we are socialised into shared norms and values, and thus culture. Neither is it the case that roles are achieved on the basis of merit. On the contrary, Marxists argue that in a capitalist system individuals are socialised into the dominant norms and values of society. Moreover, the base-superstructure model implies that the dominant norms and values of society are those of the ruling classes, since the culture, which is part of the superstructure of society, inevitably reflects the base. This is one way of interpreting Marx's comment that 'in every society the ruling ideas are always those of the ruling class', since one definition of culture is to see it as the ideas which hold a society together.

Therefore culture can be seen in terms of Marxist theory as something which does indeed act so as to bind society together. This of course, is identical to the functionalist view, which saw culture as a means of integrating society. However, the difference between Marxism and functionalism here, is that Marxism sees culture as the ideas of the ruling classes, which act so as to maintain and reproduce a capitalist society.

However, whilst Marxists see culture as an ideological device, there are several different views within Marxism as to how ideology functions. The work of **Louis Althusser** provides a useful starting point in examining these views. Althusser argued that capitalist societies required to be reproduced and controlled, and that this was achieved by means of a dominant ideology. Individuals were socialised into the dominant ideology by a variety of institutions. Althusser claimed that the dominant ideology was maintained by two structures:

- Ideological state apparatuses (ISAs)
- Repressive state apparatuses (RSAs).

Social control is much more effective when it is self-imposed, and thus the functions of the ISAs are vital in capitalist societies. Institutions such as the family, schools, religion and the mass media, form the ISAs. Should they fail to maintain social control, capitalist states must employ the RSAs, which consist of the armed forces, police and state intelligence services. This provides a very structural view of how ideology functions. Individuals appear as puppet like, with little ability to think for themselves, or to question the dominant ideology. Another group of Marxists developed a view of ideology with a broadly similar outlook, but with an explicit focus on culture. This group of scholars are known as the Frankfurt School.

CULTURE AND THE FRANKFURT SCHOOL

The Frankfurt School was a group of German sociologists working from Frankfurt University in the 1920s and 30s. Prominent members of the school included **Theodore Adorno, Max Horkheimer,** and **Herbert Marcuse.** Most of the well known members of the group were German Jews and they and the School moved to the USA when the Nazi regime came to power in Germany in the 1930s.

Whilst they were strongly influenced by Marx, the Frankfurt School were highly critical of many aspects of Marxism. Marxist theory had suggested that the working class in capitalist societies would eventually become a revolutionary political force. The Frankfurt School however, were critical of this notion, especially in the light of their experiences of the USA. In the USA the Frankfurt School observed life in a capitalist society where even the working classes seemed to have a fairly high standard of living, with a wide range of consumer goods available to many, and a culture industry providing cheap leisure and entertainment to the masses. Having experienced life in such a society, the Marxist idea of working class revolution came to seem unrealistic to them, for as they saw it, the American working classes had been incorporated into capitalist society and values, seduced by the false and shallow attractions of mass culture. In such a capitalist society, the working class would support the status quo. An escapist mass culture, such as that of the Hollywood film industry, television sitcoms, and even newspaper horoscopes, would distract the population from a concern with important social issues, and deceive them with distorted messages. These would convince people that they too could be rich, that their luck might change one day, or convince them that romance would solve all their problems.

The Frankfurt sociologists thus devised a new theory of the role of culture in capitalist societies. They saw culture as providing a meaningless distraction from the problems of everyday life. Drawing on the concepts of commodity fetishism, they argued that mass culture was best seen as an ideology, acting as a smokescreen, obscuring the true nature of existence in capitalist societies. In this way the Frankfurt School saw mass culture as an ideology and a means of social control, acting to perpetuate and stabilise capitalist society.

Study point

- Suggest why audiences may watch soap operas or listen to pop music. What criticisms can be made of the view that the audience are simply being distracted from the harsh realities of everyday life, and that mass culture is just a form of social control?

Criticisms of the Frankfurt School

Several criticisms have been levelled at the Frankfurt School's views on the role of mass culture in capitalist society. All sociologists are influenced by their own background and values. It can be argued that the Frankfurt School ultimately reflected the values and prejudices of their own class, the educated middle classes, in seeing mass culture as cheap, facile and dehumanising.

The Frankfurt School's theory of mass culture can also be seen as a version of a dominant ideology theory. It assumed that mass culture could be used as a means of social control. As **Abercrombie, Hill** and **Turner** have argued, such a thesis requires empirical evidence to support it. They argue that there is little evidence to support the sweeping claims of the dominant ideology thesis, and point to evidence which shows that dominant ideologies are always subjected to criticism and counter-ideologies. Studies of folk and popular culture in nineteenth and twentieth century America (and indeed elsewhere) show how the dominant ideology was criticised, rather than being passively accepted. **Michael Haralambos**'s study of the tradition of gospel and blues music for instance, shows how the black population used their own musical forms to express an alternative set of values. **Theodore Roszack**'s *The Making of a Counter Culture* studied the way in which the hippie movement of the 1960s rejected mainstream values.

More recently the controversial development of rap music, which is seen to represent the aggressive values of a more militant generation of inner city blacks in the USA, also indicates that Americans are hardly passive consumers of mass culture. However, these findings are compatible with a more sophisticated version of Marxism which has developed in Europe.

CULTURE, HEGEMONY AND NEO-MARXISM

Antonio Gramsci was an Italian political scientist active in the early twentieth century. He was also actively engaged in Italian political life, and was imprisoned by the dictator Mussolini in the 1920s.

Gramsci developed a theory of ideology and culture which has become very influential amongst Neo-Marxists, and was popularised in Britain by the work of Stuart Hall and the University of Birmingham's Centre for Contemporary Cultural Studies (CCCS). Gramsci recognised that culture in capitalist societies was more complex than traditional Marxist theory implied. Gramsci noted the existence of a variety of cultures within capitalist societies, but argued that one set of values, those of the ruling classes, would be dominant. He was at pains to stress that this does not imply the absence of other oppositional or counter-cultures, something which traditional Marxist theory tends to suggest. Gramsci used the term 'hegemony', meaning dominance or leadership, to refer to the idea that one culture would be seen as superior to others in a society. Indeed, Gramsci argued that alternative cultures were needed, since by permitting them to exist, the capitalist system is legitimated. It thus appears to be a fair system, precisely because it does permit the existence of alternative views.

This means that the ruling classes' cultural and ideological dominance will always be contested. Nevertheless, they could attempt to marginalise and ridicule minority views, beliefs and culture. However, by tolerating minority beliefs and culture to some extent, by for instance, not ruling them illegal, hegemony would be strengthened, since it legitimates the dominant culture.

Stuart Hall has argued that the working classes are able to resist the dominance of the ruling ideology and that this resistance can take a cultural form. Various youth subcultures such as punks, rastas and skinheads, can all be understood as developing in resistance to the culture of the dominant classes.

CULTURE, PRODUCTION AND CAPITALISM

Other sociologists influenced by Marxism have maintained a focus on what is termed the political economy of capitalism. **Golding** and **Murdock** for instance have argued that a Marxist analysis of popular or mass culture should focus on the empirical task of analysing the ownership and control of the mass media and the culture industry, and analyse the implications that this has for the production and consumption of mass culture.

Analysis of ownership and control of the mass media, indicates that, contrary to pluralist theories which claim that 'the public get what the public want' and that consumers have the power continually to exert influence on the culture industry, the production and consumption of culture is, like everything else in capitalist society, stratified on the basis of class. This is not to deny that the public has choice in the cultural products which it buys and uses, but it is to deny that all consumers, and all cultures, are equal.

Ownership of the mass media as well as the 'culture industry', which includes publishers, record companies and film companies, is restricted to a relatively small number of large corporations. For instance, many of the films produced in the world come from Hollywood. There are well known examples of large corporations dominating this area of business, including Rupert Murdoch's media empire – News International, the Walt Disney Corporation, and Time-Warner, who own a range of companies in film, music, publishing and television.

Marxists adopting a political economy approach would thus argue that such a restriction of ownership has particular effects on the production and consumption of mass culture. It can restrict and structure the nature of cultural products, since production will always be geared to the needs of corporations to make profit. This can lead to a tendency to conformity. For instance music companies may want to sign Indie bands to provide what the market wants. However, bands which are signed up may well find themselves locked into a contract which demands several recordings and eventually, over time, they may have to make artistic compromises to keep the recording company happy. Recording companies frequently repackage and reinvent their artists, attempting to sell them to another audience and thus prolong their career and profitability.

Marxists of this persuasion could also point to similar mechanisms in the field of films, where the dictates of taste in Hollywood determine the choices of cinema-goers throughout the rest of the world, or even the example of how the interests of television companies have changed the nature of many sports. Examples here include the prevalence of advertising on players' shirts in football, changing the rules of the game to make it more appealing to a television audience in the case of Rugby Union, and as Paul Manning has noted in the case of Rugby League, changing the season when the game is played!

Study point

- List the ways in which restricted ownership has recently affected cultural production in either the media, entertainment, or leisure businesses.

The point Marxists are making about these sorts of changes is that rather than reflecting popular opinion and acting to extend choice, they represent the interests of large corporations, and they result in less choice. They also illustrate a basic idea in Marxism, that all activities become commodified. Moreover, Marxists taking this view argue that the choices people make in participating in cultural activities are constrained by economic structures. Emphasis of this point distinguishes the political economist approach in Marxism from the view of theorists such as Gramsci and the Frankfurt School, who at times seem to envisage people freely choosing which cultural activities they will participate in. The political economy approach in Marxism has less to say about the ideological effects of culture, some theorists prefering to leave this an open question to be investigated.

Activity

Using CD-Rom or documentary sources, conduct research into the ownership and control of the media, entertainment or leisure industries. Identify some of the major companies in these business areas and the interests and companies which they own. Discuss the implications this may have for the consumer.

CRITICISMS OF THE MARXIST APPROACH TO CULTURE

Briefly two main criticisms can be made of all Marxist approaches to culture. Marxist theories can be seen as being:

- economically reductionist;
- too structural.

By the term economic reductionism, critics mean that Marxism tends to see all cultural activity as being a response to economic factors and conditions, and as always reflecting the class relationships inherent within a society. It can be argued that Marxism thus exaggerates the importance of class and the economy. Critics might point out for example, that popular culture could reflect religious beliefs prevalent in a society, or simply other aspects of the beliefs and ideas of a community. Critics argue that the economy does not determine all other structures and relationships within a society, and that ideas and culture can be autonomous from the economy and class structure.

Marxism is of course, a structural theory, and the criticisms and issues raised in the debates between structural and action approaches are of relevance here. Critics can fairly point out that Marxist accounts of culture and identity appear to leave no room for individual choice; human beings can appear to be objects who act in accordance with the demands of the class structure. There is little recognition in some versions of Marxism that individuals may actually play a part in creating culture.

CLASS, CULTURE AND CAPITALISM — AN EVALUATION

The main points which Marxism makes about culture may be briefly stated:

* Ruling class values determine the dominant cultural values.
* The working class is provided with a culture which deludes and entertains and inhibits reflection and criticism.
* Cultural norms are imposed as a form of social control.

It is possible to identify over-simplifications and exaggerations in the Marxist analysis of culture. Nevertheless it is Marxism which, because of its focus on power and inequality, can point out how the concept of culture is used evaluatively and ideologically.

SUMMARY

Both Marxism and functionalism, in offering a structural view of culture and identity can provide a view of society, individuals, and culture and identity, which appears to make people look rather mechanical or robotic. Many sociologists, even those who are fans of Marxism or functionalism, have been unhappy with this aspect of the theories. An alternative to both of these structural views of culture and identity comes from the sociological perspective called interactionism. The views of this perspective will be discussed in the next chapter.

STUDY GUIDES

1 In groups construct an evaluation chart (see introduction) of Marxist theories of culture and identity. Once each group has finished, pool your ideas, and individually try to produce your own brief concluding statement, evaluating the strengths and weaknesses of Marxist theories.

2 Conduct a debate on the motion that 'Mass Culture operates as a form of social control which the masses are unable to resist'.

3 Draw up a list of questions on the Marxist approach to culture and identity which you would like to present to Karl Marx. Cut up the questions, place them into a hat (or similar object), and ask your teacher to take the role of Karl Marx. Then proceed with the interview.

Practice Questions

ITEM A

The ideas of the ruling class are, in every age, the ruling ideas: i.e. the class which is the dominant material force in society is at the same time its dominant intellectual force.

Karl Marx, The German Ideology, in Bottomore and Rubel, Selected Writings in Sociology and Social Philosophy, 1990, p93

ITEM B

Ideology then refers to a system of beliefs characteristic of a particular class or group. Ideological forms are not only ideas, cultural values and religious beliefs, but also their embodiment in cultural institutions (schools, churches, art galleries, legal systems, political parties), and in cultural artifacts (texts, paintings, buildings and so on). This broad definition of ideology clearly includes the arts and culture. The cultural producer has his or her own location in the social structure, potentially generating its own ideological form; but at the same time, the society as a whole will be characterised by general ideological forms arising out of general economic conditions and the mode of production of that society. For instance, John Berger's interpretation of Gainsborough's painting *Mr and Mrs Andrews*, suggests that the landscape, recognisably the property of the Andrews, is not an accidental feature, dependent purely on the artists inclination, but integral to the commission. Berger comments, 'Among the pleasures their portrait gave to Mr and Mrs Andrews was the pleasure of seeing themselves depicted as landowners and this pleasure was enhanced by the ability of oil paint to render their land in all its substantiality'.

Janet Woolf, The Social Production of Art, Macmillan 1993, p55–56

1   Explain how the Marxist view of ruling class ideology described in Item A can be applied to the topic of culture and identity.   (4)
2   Using material from elsewhere, briefly describe the approach of the Frankfurt School to popular or mass culture.   (6)
3   With reference to Item B, explain how it is that Marxists can describe an artistic activity such as painting as an 'ideological form'.   (6)
4   Evaluate Marxist approaches to the study of culture and identity, with particular reference to popular culture.   (9)

Coursework

1   Examine the theories of the Frankfurt School. What evidence is there to support the view that mass culture acts ideologically, as a means of social control?
2   Compare and contrast changes in private and public broadcasting in recent years. Consider factors such as management style, advertising, sources of funding and revenue, and programming. Apply Marxist concepts and the political economy approach to assess the effects and implications of changes in ownership and control of the media. Use information from the national and specialist press to provide evidence of recent changes.
3   Investigate the extent to which working class culture and cultural activity can be seen as a form of 'resistance'. Examine for instance, cultural activity such as football, pop music, or popular television programmes.

5

CULTURE, IDENTITY AND THE INTERPRETIVE PERSPECTIVE

Introduction

THE TERM 'the interpretive perspective' applies to a range of sociological theories the most important of which are symbolic interactionism and ethnomethodology. Sociologists frequently use terms such as 'social action theory' or 'interactionism' in a general sense to refer to the broad concerns of this tradition of theory. All of these different versions of interpretive theories have in common the idea that sociology should concern itself with explaining the interactions which occur between the individual and society. Applying this general idea to culture and identity, interpretivist theories would suggest that culture has to be seen as a process, rather than a rigid structure. According to this view, culture is the outcome of a process of negotiation. Cultural rules, or norms and values, may often be disputed, neglected, or misunderstood. This means that there will be a variety of interpretations of norms and values, leading to differing subcultural adaptations to the culture. In terms of the symbolic aspects of culture, whilst there are some shared meanings, such as language, meanings are often interpreted in different ways.

Interpretive theories are very much modern theories of society, but their historical origins are complex. Two important sociologists in the interpretivist tradition are the German sociologists, **Max Weber** and **Georg Simmel**. Weber's work stressed the need for sociology to understand the reasons individuals gave for their actions. Simmel expressed a broadly similar view, arguing that society should be seen as consisting of interactions between individuals. However, much of the history of interpretive theory in the twentieth century is dominated by

American sociologists and the schools of thought known as symbolic interactionism and ethnomethodology. The contribution of interactionist theory can be seen as owing much to the environment in which it was developed, though this comment can be made as a criticism. This chapter will examine and critically evaluate the contribution which interpretive theory can make to understanding culture and identity.

Table 4: *Theorists, concepts and issues in this chapter*		
KEY THEORISTS	KEY CONCEPTS	KEY ISSUES
• G H Mead	Self-concept	To what extent are culture and identity created by skilled actors rather than structural forces?
• Howard Becker	Labelling	
• Erving Goffman	Stigmatised identity	Why are some identities more highly regarded than others?
• Rosenthal and Jacobsen	Negotiated order	How are deviant identities socially created?
• David Matza	Indexicality	
• Harold Garfinkel	Reflexivity	
• Aaron Cicourel	Glossing	
	Total institutions	

IDENTITY, SELF AND SOCIETY

THE CHICAGO SCHOOL

For the Chicago School sociologists, the cities of North America appeared to be characterised by a lack of community and rootlessness; they were societies of strangers. For some members of the Chicago School this led to a focus on urban society and culture, whilst others, such as **G H Mead**, **Charles Cooley**, and **Herbert Blumer**, were concerned to explain how modern society created such a culture and the identity that went with it. It is from these roots that symbolic interactionism developed.

For G H Mead the distinguishing feature of human society is the fact that human beings create and communicate meanings through the use of symbols. The most common system of symbols is of course language, but other forms of activity or object may become symbolic and thus transmit meanings, such as music, clothing, or body language or gestures. Mead argued that our sense of self is the result of interaction with others. This idea is often misinterpreted or over-simplified. Mead did not suggest that individuals interact simply 'with society', nor was he claiming that society consists solely of individuals (individualism).

Mead argued that our sense of self was developed through the interaction between our self-concept and the view which others have of us. Mead saw the self, or the individual, as consisting of two parts, and used the terms 'I' and 'Me' to refer to these two parts. The 'I' refers to the idea of how an individual sees him or herself, and the 'Me' how others see them. For Mead, this makes the self, the individual's identity, a process. The self is developed in interaction with others. Mead argues that individuals learn to take roles by interpreting how others – or 'generalised others' – respond. By the term 'generalised others', Mead refers to the wider society in general. Individuals may also be influenced by 'significant others', which refers to the role taken by parents, or any other people who become important and act as role models to an individual. Mead's view is that an individual's self-identity is gradually learnt and internalised (it becomes a part of us). In Mead's terms, the individual learns to 'take on the role of the generalised other'; in other words, individuals gradually learn to see themselves in the roles which the rest of society sees them as occupying. So for example, individuals gradually learn and internalise the roles expected of men and women.

Mead's terminology is not always easy to grasp, but the essence of his view of the self is captured in the term devised by Charles Cooley, 'the looking glass self'. What Mead and Cooley were drawing attention to here, is the way in which human behaviour is moulded by the reactions of others. Mead and Cooley are suggesting that an individual's actions will meet with either positive or negative sanctioning from peers. Individuals will learn to see themselves as others see them, and thus will internalise the values of the social groups which they are members of. However, this is a process, since individuals have to interpret the meanings and intentions which lie behind the responses of others.

Study point

- Give examples of the ways in which people's self-image can be influenced by the judgements of others. How can this influence the identity of the individual?

SYMBOLIC INTERACTIONISM

Herbert Blumer, who studied as a student under G H Mead at the University of Chicago, developed and systematised the ideas of Mead and Cooley, and was responsible for inventing the term 'symbolic interactionism'. Blumer famously summarised the views of symbolic interactionism in three main points:

- people act on the basis of meanings;
- meanings are the product of social interaction between people;
- meanings are continually being modified and therefore have to be interpreted.

The emphasis which symbolic interactionists place on meaning, and the role which individuals play in creating meaning, shows a clear link with the theoretical concerns of Weber and Simmel. Interactionists carried on with this focus on meaning and the questions it raised about what processes are involved in creating the individual characteristic of modern society. Action and interaction within society are seen as the result of shared meanings. It is only because meanings are shared that social life is possible. Learning to be a member of a society means learning a culture, and that in turn involves becoming a skilled user of shared meanings, whether they be expressed in terms of language or other symbol systems, such as body language for instance. Symbolic interactionism thus presents a view of culture which starts with an assumption common to functionalist theory – the assumption of shared meanings. However, symbolic interactionism proceeds to argue that culture is not the rigid structure which functionalists describe. On the contrary, culture is a process, and meanings, roles, norms and values are best seen as flexible processes, and as things which are created by people. This is not to say however, that the process of creating culture, roles, and identity, is always one which works to the advantage of all, as functionalists would argue. A development within interactionist theory has argued that some identities and roles result from the negative reaction of society, (the generalised other). This development is called labelling theory.

Study point
• Discuss the symbolic meaning of the following items: the national flag, traffic lights, a football club shirt, badges. Do these symbols always have the same meaning for all individuals?

LABELLING THEORY, IDENTITY AND SOCIETY

Labelling theory contributed to the development of interactionist theory through the realisation that by adjusting the focus of symbolic interactionism, further insights could be made. Rather than focus upon the individual and the self, labelling theory suggested that the focus should be upon society's reaction to the individual. **Howard Becker**, one of the pioneers of labelling theory, conducted considerable research into the topic of deviance, or behaviour which does not conform to norms and values.

Becker famously defined deviance as follows:

> *Social groups create deviance by making the rules whose infraction constitutes deviance, and by applying those rules to particular people and labelling them as outsiders. From this point of view, deviance is not a quality of the act the person commits, but rather a consequence of the application by others of the rules and sanctions to an offender. The deviant is one to whom the label has successfully been applied; deviant behaviour is behaviour that people so label.*

It is important here to distinguish between crime and deviance. Crime refers to acts which are against the law, and which will be formally sanctioned, whereas deviance refers to all acts which break social norms and values. Becker argues that whether an act is defined as deviant or criminal will depend on the situation and will vary between different societies. Definitions of deviant and criminal acts will also vary over time, as society and values change.

For Becker however, the point is that it is society which plays the key role in applying a negative label to individuals who are seen to fail to conform to social norms and values. Becker argues that certain labels can have a 'master status', that is they outweigh all other roles or identities that an individual may have. So for example, the labels thief, drug addict, alcoholic, gay, disabled, mentally ill, murderer, are all 'master statuses'.

Becker explains that it is society which creates deviance, not the individual, since the negative reaction of society to individual behaviour sets the individual out on a path which reinforces the offending behaviour, and in effect pushes them out to the margins of society. The deviant career, as Becker calls it, commences with the initial labelling of behaviour, which leads to a rejection from other social groups (work, family, education). The common experience of those imprisoned provides a good example. Once defined as a criminal, it is hard to get a job, and soon the individual may commit further deviant behaviour, leading perhaps to further imprisonment or punishment. However, this simply reinforces the negative label. Ultimately the individual defined as deviant is likely to join a deviant group or subculture. This, Becker argues, is quite a logical step, for the individual so labelled, is in fact largely driven out from the wider society, and joining a group where ones actions are approved of provides support and protection from the wider society. Becker has studied how this process occurs in the case of marijuana users and jazz musicians. The title of Becker's book, *Outsiders*, underlines the point that deviant subcultures are forced, to some degree at least, to live outside the norms and values of the wider society.

Becker's ideas have been usefully reflected and adapted in a range of sociological work. Labelling has had a particularly strong influence in the study of crime and deviance, and in the sociology of education. An example worth noting here, is the concept of the self-fulfilling prophecy, used by **Rosenthal** and **Jacobsen** in their study of interaction between teachers and pupils. Rosenthal and Jacobsen's study suggested that teachers' assessments of students' ability influenced students in subtle ways. The result of such assessments was that those students perceived to be more able did in fact achieve higher levels than those perceived less positively by their teachers. Findings such as these, along with Becker's work, suggest that the concept of labelling has much to contribute to the study of culture and identity. Becker's work in particular illustrates how culture, both in terms of a shared way of life, and in terms of shared meanings, is something which is socially constructed. However, it also raises questions about the relationship between culture and subculture, and indeed, about the nature and role of culture. These issues are the subject of the next section.

Study point

- Suggest criticisms which could be made of labelling theory and the self-fulfilling prophecy.

Activity

Conduct research into the use of sexist language and the debate over 'political correctness', by examining the ethical guidelines of the British Sociological Association (BSA), and the 'Notes for Contributors' in the BSA journal, *Sociology*. A questionnaire could also be devised for a survey conducted to investigate attitudes towards issues of sexist language and political correctness. Is sexist language a form of labelling? What effect might it have upon individual identity? What conclusions could be drawn about British culture if sexist language is prevalent and accepted by large numbers of the population?

CULTURE, SUBCULTURE AND NEGOTIATED ORDER

The sociologist **David Matza** has argued for caution in assuming that deviant subcultures reject in a radical sense the norms and values of the wider society. Matza argues that in fact, deviant subcultures simply alter the priorities of the wider common culture of society, or focus on particular aspects and particular intepretations of the common culture. Thus the subculture of football hooligans, which accords a central role to violence, does so in the context of a wider culture which also stresses the importance of courage, manliness, standing up for yourself, independence and loyalty to one's community. Whilst the subculture of football hooligans interprets these values in an exaggerated way, they are arguably, at least recognisable as part of the wider culture.

In the hands of interactionist and interpretivist sociologists, culture has come to be seen as something which is much more flexible than structural theories have implied. Culture is seen to be a process, and identity and roles as things which are fluid and mouldable, rather than set in stone. All sociologists influenced by interpretivist theory would generally agree that culture does act as a flexible structure or guide for action, but would wish to emphasise that cultural norms and values, roles and identities, are created by people, who must be seen as active and creative beings. This, however, is not to neglect the idea that culture can be used by certain groups in society, as is hinted at in interactionist theory, not least through the concept of labelling.

'Moral entrepreneurs'

- Howard Becker for instance has argued that interactionist studies of deviance do indeed need to examine carefully not just the labelled, but those who do the labelling. Becker terms these 'moral entrepreneurs'. Becker's notion of moral entrepreneurs has been taken up in work by British sociologists **Stan Cohen** and **Jock Young**. Cohen's famous study, *Folk Devils and Moral Panics*, focused on the fights between rival youth groups – mods and rockers in the 1960s. Cohen demonstrates how the action of police, courts and mass media, through exaggerated reporting, created what he terms a 'moral panic'. Cohen argues that the initial disturbances were minor, and that subsequent media reporting and police action led to the provocation of further incidents and an escalation of disorder. Groups such as the mods and rockers found themselves placed in the role of 'outsiders', to use Becker's term, and were seen as a threat to established norms and values. Cohen thus describes the youths as becoming seen as 'folk devils', a perceived danger to the culture.

'Deviance amplification'

- Jock Young's study of drug culture in London's Notting Hill area, similarly demonstrates the way in which the identification and labelling of a group can exacerbate a perceived problem. Young terms this 'deviance amplification', and argues that police action against drug users in the area, in fact led to the creation of an even more notable drug subculture. This is similar in many ways to the processes of labelling described by Becker. In these examples, the 'moral entrepreneurs' could be seen as the police, courts, and media.

Both of these studies, and indeed the interactionist approach to culture and subculture, in turn had an influence on work by Marxist sociologist **Stuart Hall** and others in the book *Policing the Crisis*. This is an important example which illustrates the way in which sociologists can draw from different theoretical traditions in their work. Hall's work examined the way in which a moral panic developed over street crime, and in particular the crime of mugging, in London during the 1970s. Despite his Marxist influences, Hall argued that this period could usefully be seen as a struggle over culture, for in this case the perceived criminals were 'black' and the moral panic which developed became exceptionally heightened as so-called 'black crime' was seen to present a threat to the whole of the perceived indigenous 'white' culture. Thus, seen as a conflict between two rival sets of cultural values, so-called 'black crime' was presented as a threat or challenge (falsely in Hall's view) to the British way of life. In this case again, the police and the media can be seen as key moral entrepreneurs.

In all of these examples, interactionists are presenting culture as a process rather than a structure. Unlike functionalists and Marxists, interactionists do not see order and social control as things which are simply imposed. On the contrary, order and social control are seen as the outcome of a process of negotiation. Whilst some sociologists have criticised labelling theory for appearing to imply that the process is automatic, other traditions within interpretivist theory have been at pains to stress the role of negotiation in creating social order: **Aaron Cicourel**'s study of juvenile crime for example, which demonstrated how the police, courts and social workers define a juvenile criminal in a particular way. Class, ethnicity and gender, amongst other factors, come into play, and the ability to escape negative labelling will frequently depend on which social groups an individual belongs to.

Activity

Use a CD-Rom to look up newspaper reports on rave and drug culture. Consider whether newspapers label young people, or drug users, and the influences which this has on identity. You could also consider in what ways rave culture or drug culture can be considered to be subcultures.

ETHNOMETHODOLOGY, IDENTITY AND THE SKILLED ACTOR

The branch of interpretivist theory which Aaron Cicourel is associated with is known as ethnomethodology. This differs from symbolic interactionism in a subtle way. Symbolic interactionism focuses on studying the processes of interaction in society. Thus symbolic interactionists will examine the way in which a person is labelled as a criminal or as a less able student. Ethnomethodologists on the other hand aim to analyse the methods which people use to make sense of and explain their society and their social practices. In these examples, that would mean that the ethnomethodologist would wish to examine what people mean by the term 'criminal', or 'student', or 'less able', and attempt to discover how the definition and application of these terms is negotiated. **Harold Garfinkel**, one of the key originators of ethnomethodology, argued that other sociological theories, including interactionism, show human beings to be what he called 'cultural dopes' – robots or puppets, who simply obeyed the rules laid down by culture. Garfinkel argued that individuals were, on the contrary, thinking and reflective beings.

Indexicality

- The concepts of indexicality, reflexivity and glossing, are particularly important in Garfinkel's account of ethnomethodology, and provide an insight into the central concerns of the theory. By indexicality, Garfinkel refers to the idea that the meaning of all words, symbols and actions used in social life depends upon the context, or the situation, in which they are used. A person uttering the words 'You're dead' for instance, will be interpreted in very different ways according to the situation. Amongst friends this remark could be simply a joking rebuke, but if the speaker is armed and in the process of robbing a building society, the meaning changes.

Reflexivity

- Reflexivity refers to the idea that in giving explanations and descriptions of social practices people are also creating or constituting the social practice. If we ask a friend what the 22 people on the grass are doing, and the reply affirms that they are playing a game of football, then this is in fact a contribution to society and social practice. We are helping to define the action we see before us as a game of football, and not as something else, eg another game, a waste of time, or a religious ceremony. Our account and explanation of society, itself becomes part of society.

Glossing

- The last concept, glossing, simply refers to the fact that in day to day social life, we do not have to give laborious explanations of what we are doing, what it means, and why we are doing it. Because we can act on the basis of indexicality and reflexivity, we can indeed take many or most things, for granted. Thus individuals give a gloss on what they are doing, an incomplete or shorthand account of their action, which they can assume will be understood correctly, due to the context. The task of sociology therefore, is to analyse the mechanisms actors use to create these meanings and social practices.

Ethnomethodology has been subject to several important criticisms, which will be discussed on p 57. Nevertheless, ethnomethodology can contribute to an understanding of culture and identity, for it provides several useful insights:

- In arguing that individuals are skilled actors, it suggests that identity is something which individuals can create, rather than having imposed upon them.
- It suggests that both culture and identity are socially constructed concepts, and encourages us to investigate how social actors go about defining and using the term culture and identity.
- Applying the concept of indexicality to culture and identity suggests that the

meaning of both terms will vary according to the context in which they are used. This can be related to the different definitions and levels of culture, such as high, low, popular, mass and folk culture.

● It points out the importance for sociologists to attempt to view taken for granted assumptions critically.

The interpretive perspective as examined thus far, however helpful it may appear to be, could be open to the criticism that it neglects the role that large institutions play in creating culture and identity in modern society. Modern society is after all, characterised by the existence of large organisations. The work of Erving Goffman attempts to provide a distinctly interactionist approach to this aspect of modern life.

INSTITUTIONS, IDENTITY AND SOCIETY

Erving Goffman's work, drawing largely on the symbolic interactionism of the Chicago School, is often referred to as presenting a dramaturgical approach to sociology. This term simply means that Goffman saw society as a theatre. The term, however, is often misinterpreted as a result of over-simplification. Careful interpretation is important here, to avoid confusing Goffman's approach with that of functionalism. Functionalists too, have sometimes seen the idea of role as akin to an actor learning a script, arguing in effect that people learn the lines needed for their role, and by and large stick to them. In this way, people's actions seem to be predetermined by the needs of social structures, and they thus appear rather like puppets, with no ability to make choices or decisions for themselves.

This is not what Goffman intends by the theatre metaphor. Rather Goffman intended to emphasise the way in which social action is always a performance and that individuals are, in some senses, always putting on an act. Just as in a theatrical production actors try to convince an audience of the reality of the performance (at least in modern theatre), people try to present a favourable image of their actions and motives in social situations. In his book *Asylums*, Goffman claims that one of his main concerns is 'to develop a sociological version of the structure of the self'.

Goffman's sociological work achieves this by presenting a thorough classification of the ways in which people try to control what Goffman terms 'the arts of impression management'. Goffman uses a variety of terms to describe the strategies individuals commonly use in this process, such as:

● front and back regions;
● dramatical realisation;
● idealisation;
● mystification.

The terms front and back regions give a good example of what the dramaturgical approach involves. In managing their behaviour people learn to present an idealised image of themselves, to present a front. Backstage, so to speak, they can relax. An example would be the way shop staff will try to be polite when dealing with customers, but in the privacy of the staff canteen will feel free to vent their true feelings. The idea of front and back regions can apply to the most apparently minor acts; Goffman would argue that actions such as going to the toilet, scratching our backside, or having a bath, are all private acts which we confine to the back region. We put on an act and prefer to give the impression that these activities do not exist when presenting ourselves in public.

Study point
• Suggest some examples of impression management. How important are these in creating identity?

Other terms such as 'dramatical realisation' and 'mystification' refer to the ways in which individuals may try to make their actions and themselves more important, and 'idealisation' refers to the ways in which people attempt to conceal errors, secret activities and other aspects of their lives which they prefer to hide.

TOTAL INSTITUTIONS

In his book *Asylums*, Goffman examines these and other strategies in the context of what he terms 'total institutions'. Goffman was interested in the processes by which an individual's concept of self was created. He was also concerned to examine the processes involved in the case of those defined as deviant, or whose identity was stigmatised in some way.

Goffman defines a total institution as any institution which deals with or treats individuals in some way, contains individuals who are seen as belonging to the institution and are barred or restricted from the wider society, and which makes clear distinctions between staff and inmates. Such a definition would mean that institutions such as mental hospitals, hospitals, monasteries, boarding schools, prisons, concentration camps and military organisations could be included in the category of total institutions. Goffman's own research was carried out in a mental hospital, but the processes he describes can be applied to other total institutions.

Goffman argues that within the confines of the total institution, individuals are subjected to a process of mortification, or a death of the self. Goffman describes how total institutions secure control over inmates by a variety of rituals and routines, such as the issuing of uniform, haircuts, the confiscation of personal belongings; even stripping, washing and medical examination can contribute to this process. All the individual's previous ability to control and define their own sense of self and identity are stripped away, and the inmate is allowed no control over even such mundane matters as what to eat, what to wear or how to spend free time. Goffman identifies several ways in which individuals adapt to this situation, including 'situational withdrawal', where the inmate simply becomes withdrawn and attempts to avoid any trouble; 'conversion', where the inmate tries to adopt and exemplify the norms and values of the institution; 'playing it cool', whereby the inmate takes a calculated approach to institutional demands, and 'plays the game', 'gives them what they want', with the ultimate objective of course of gaining what the inmate wants: release. Goffman describes the whole process involved in becoming an inmate as a 'moral career', since the different stages he identifies form a progression. At the end of the process the individual may be released from the institution, but as Goffman notes, they may often experience difficulty in coping with the culture of life outside an institution. Moreover the individual may then find themselves having a stigmatised identity. In a similar way to the idea of master status, the ex-inmate will find that their identity is one which is responded to negatively.

Study point

- Discuss to what extent schools may be regarded as total institutions.

Goffman's contribution to the interactionist perspective is useful for several reasons:

- It shows us the strategies which people may use in creating and maintaining a certain self-identity.
- It shows how institutions can act so as to change people's sense of self and their identity. This is an idea which could be adapted and extended to other types of institutions, such as schools or factories. Institutions can exert social control in a very powerful manner, even controlling a person's sense of identity.

The interpretive perspective, and the particular contributions from symbolic interactionism and ethnomethodology, may be seen as having provided a much needed alternative to structural theories. Nevertheless, like all theories they have their critics, and it is now necessary to consider some of the main criticisms aimed at the interpretive perspective and its approach to culture and identity.

CRITICISMS OF THE INTERPRETIVE PERSPECTIVE

There are several main criticisms which are levelled at the interpretive perspective. These will be dealt with in a general way here, since many criticisms can apply to the range of interpretive theories.

- It is trivial. Interactionist and ethnomethodological studies are sometimes said to be statements of the obvious, requiring no special skill or knowledge, and are certainly not scientific. More pejoratively, interactionism has been referred to as the study of 'nuts 'n' sluts', because of its followers' penchant for observing deviant groups and subcultures.
- It is descriptive rather than explanatory. Echoing the comments above, sociology becomes simply descriptive journalism.
- It neglects power and the social structures which create it. Whilst there is a great deal of interest in how cultural meanings are constructed, and how interaction occurs between individuals, there is no consideration of where meanings come from. Who makes the cultural rules (norms and values) which determine how actions and meanings can be interpreted?
- It's popularity and development in the USA suggests that the focus on individuals in fact means that interactionism and ethnomethodology simply reflect the dominant ideology of the USA. This ideology is individualistic, and fails to situate the individual in social context, thus neglecting structures of power, such as class, ethnicity and gender.
- Labelling theory can be seen as deterministic. It seems to imply that once a label has been attached the individual has no ability to reject the label.

EVALUATION

Some of the most important criticisms of interpretivist theories focus on the perspective's supposed lack of scientific rigour. Interpretivists deliberately avoid supposedly scientific methods since they see these as obscuring the reality of social relations. Rather than use survey methods to study crime for instance, interpretivists argue that it is more useful to see why people get involved in crime, or ask people what they mean by crime and what makes a crime distinct from other actions. Goffman's study of mental hospital patients for instance, would perhaps have been much less revealing had he used a questionnaire format, rather than the participant observation which he actually conducted.

Research in the interpretive tradition has also been seen as being trivial or sensationalist. Triviality is often a criticism made of ethnomethodologists, particularly Garfinkel's studies. However, given some of the use of interpretivist theory in the areas of crime, deviance and education, this seems a harsh, unfair, and even ignorant, judgement. Research in these areas can have direct implications for social policies. Frequently those making this sort of criticism have a different conception of sociology, wishing it to attempt to emulate the natural sciences. Additionally, it could be noted that those who parody interpretivist work as the study of 'nuts 'n' sluts', demonstrate yet again the inevitable value-laden nature of sociological work. Values will determine not just how we study, but what we study. In the area of culture and identity, this is as important as ever, and these comments remind us of how difficult it is to study the things closest to us with a degree of objectivity.

The criticisms made in terms of power and ideology are perhaps easier to sympathise with. However, it can be argued that to claim that interactionist theories neglect power is to misinterpret them to some degree. Work by sociologists such as Becker, Cicourel and Goffman has on the contrary raised key issues of power. Cicourel's work for instance, has tried to force American society to ask itself difficult questions about how its law and order system works. Becker has shown how powerful institutions in American society have criminalised the use of marijuana. Goffman's study of how institutions create particular types of identity must surely be concerned with issues of power by definition.

Some critics, though, have felt that in labelling theory the issue of power is all too clear and that it is in one direction, from labeller to victim. This may be how labelling theory appears in some studies, such as those of Rosenthal and Jacobsen for instance. On the whole, however, interactionists have been concerned to emphasise the very point that labelling is a process, as indeed the work of Goffman illustrates by showing how mental hospital patients try to avoid the attempts of the institution to 'mortify' their sense of self.

Nevertheless, it is perhaps less contentious to argue that power and structure is not dealt with adequately in interpretivist theories. As the criticism described above indicates, the question of where definitions, labels, meanings and identities, come from has to be addressed, and this is a weak point in interactionist theories. It does not mean however that the approach is without value, or that it cannot be adapted. Ultimately the strengths and weaknesses of sociological theories tend to reflect their position in regard to the structure/action debate. Interpretivist theory is, of course, clearly on the action side, and so it is not surprising to find weaknesses when one comes to consider structure.

APPLICATIONS

The interpretivist approach has much to say about culture and identity. It can usefully be applied to the different categories and definitions of culture, such as high, mass or popular culture. Interpretivist theories would encourage investigation of what the various terms mean, how they are used and constructed by different groups within society, who defines them and how they influence identity. One could also consider whether and how culture involves labelling processes, or examine cultural values and the stigmatising of certain groups:

class, ethnicity, gender, age or region. Sociological studies such as **Sue Lees'** book *Sugar and Spice,* show how a male dominated culture influences the identity of girls, while **Paul Willis**'s study *Learning to Labour* argues that anti-school subculture becomes a preparation for factory culture.

Activity
Conduct a piece of research to discover how 'reputational labelling' differs between males and females. Discuss whether and how reputational labelling may act as a form of social control, and what effects it may have upon identity. How does reputational labelling reflect cultural values?

SUMMARY

Interactionist or interpretive approaches to culture and identity clearly have much to offer the sociologist. However, despite their differences all the theories considered up to this point can be referred to as modernist theories. The next three chapters proceed to examine how modernist theories have understood the relationship between culture and identity, and class, gender and ethnicity. In doing this, the various criticisms made of modernist sociology will be considered.

Group Work

1 Produce an evaluation chart to summarise interactionist approaches to culture and identity. Make your own individual summary and compare with the rest of the group.

2 Make a list of the pros and cons of structural and action approaches to culture and identity. Ensure that you conclude the debate.

3 In three groups construct a list of key concepts (see introduction) and key studies discussed so far. Each group should deal with one theory (Functionalist, Marxist, and Interpretivist). If numbers allow, a fourth group could do the same for sociobiological theories.

Practice Questions

ITEM A

At our destination we were met by hundreds and hundreds of police, who then escorted us to the ground by a circuitous route away from the city centre; it was during these walks that my urban hooligan fantasies were given free rein. I was completely safe, protected not only by the law but by my fellow supporters, and I had therefore been liberated to bellow along in my still unbroken voice with the chanted threats of the others. I didn't look terribly hard, in truth: I was as yet nowhere near as big as I should have been, and wore black-framed Brains-style National Health reading glasses, although these I hid away for the duration of the route marches, presumably to make myself just that little bit more terrifying. But those who mumble about the loss of identity football fans must endure miss the point: this loss of identity can be a paradoxically enriching process. Who wants to be stuck with who they are the whole time? I for one wanted time out from being a jug-eared, bespectacled, suburban twerp once in a while; I loved being able to frighten the shoppers in Derby or Norwich or Southampton (and they were frightened – you could see it).

Nick Hornby, Fever Pitch, Indigo 1996, p54

ITEM B

All social groups make rules and attempt, at some times and under some circumstances, to enforce them. Social rules define situations and the kinds of behaviour appropriate to them, specifying some actions as 'right' and forbidding others as 'wrong'. When a rule is enforced, the person who is supposed to have broken it may be seen as a special kind of person, one who cannot be trusted to live by the rules agreed upon by the group. He is regarded as an outsider.

But the person who is thus labelled an outsider may have a different view of the matter. He may not accept the rule by which he is being judged and may not regard those who judge him as either competent or legitimately entitled to do so. Hence, a second meaning of the term emerges: the rule-breaker may feel his judges are outsiders.

Howard Becker, Outsiders, The Free Press (Macmillan) 1963, p1–2

1   In what ways can the information in Item A be seen to support an interactionist view of identity?   (8)

2   Item B suggests that a person who breaks society's rules becomes an outsider.
    (i) What terms other than 'outsider' do sociologists use to describe the identity of such persons   (2)
    (ii) Give two examples of such forms of identity.   (2)

3   With reference to Item B, identify the methodological problems which may be raised by sociologists' attempts to define the concept of culture?   (4)

4   Evaluate the contribution which interactionism makes to an understanding of culture and identity, using information from the Items and elsewhere.   (9)

Coursework

1   Use Goffman's concepts and theories to examine the effects of various types of institution (eg schools, hospitals, factories or large organisations) upon identity.

2   Conduct a study into reputational labelling and examine how stigmatised identities or labels influence identity.

3   Study the way in which people in a particular social context use impression management. You could study a school, workplace, or a leisure activity which you are involved in. Is impression management effective in creating a particular identity, and what functions does it serve?

6

CULTURE, IDENTITY AND CLASS

Introduction

FOR MUCH OF the twentieth century sociologists agreed that modern societies were, above all, class societies. This view is now coming under increasing criticism, and for some it does seem that class is a less important aspect in the way individuals think of themselves. Nevertheless it can be argued that sociologists cannot dispense with the concept of class, for it continues to have a profound effect on modern industrial culture, and, arguably, class remains an important influence upon identity. Rather than dispense with the concept of class, sociologists may suggest that we need to ask questions about the relationship between class and culture. Sociologists are for instance concerned with the question of whether distinct cultural practices can be associated with particular classes; is there a distinctive working class culture, and a distinct middle class culture, and if there is, what social effects do they have?

More recently sociologists have also raised questions about how class may be related to the production and consumption of cultural activities, such as music, literature and the various products of the mass media, such as films and television programmes. In this area of study, sociologists have been interested in asking questions about how culture is produced, who produces it, and about who uses it and how. Sociologists are interested in the process whereby cultural practices, activities and products are judged and evaluated by society; are some cultural practices and products seen as superior to others, and if so why? These are difficult questions to answer, not least because culture is a contested concept. This chapter will examine the various ways in which sociologists have attempted to answer these questions.

Table 5: *Theorists, concepts and issues in this chapter*		
KEY THEORISTS	KEY CONCEPTS	KEY ISSUES
• E P Thompson	Class culture	What influence does class have upon identity?
• Richard Hoggart	Mass/popular culture	Do classes have distinct cultures?
• The Frankfurt School	High culture	Does class have less influence upon identity in contemporary society?
• Walter Benjamin	Folk culture	
• Pierre Bourdieu	Dependency cultures	What is the role of class and class culture in defining cultural tastes?
• Charles Murray	Cultural deprivation	Are some cultures better than others?
• Peter Saunders		
• Dick Hebdige	Cultural capital	Do the differences between high culture and mass culture reflect the class structure?
• John Clarke	Habitus	
• Centre for Contemporary Cultural Studies (CCCS)	Cultural production	
• Ien Ang	Cultural populism	

MODERNITY, CLASS AND CULTURE

The effects of industrialisation and capitalism upon society generally, have been discussed previously (see Chapters 3 and 4). However, the cultural effects of the transformation of pre-industrial society require further discussion. The work of the social historian **E P Thompson** and cultural critics such as **Richard Hoggart**, are of particular interest to sociologists.

E P Thompson's historical work was concerned with the effects of industrialisation upon the traditional pre-industrial labouring classes. Thompson's historical work provides a vivid portrait of the process by which the pre-industrial way of life of labouring people was destroyed by industrialisation. Even the most apparently mundane aspects of life, such as concepts of time were transformed by the industrial culture. As Thompson illustrates, the change to urban living and factory work required new habits of timekeeping and discipline from the working population. It was no longer possible to work when one chose, to fit work to the seasons and the elements. Industrial capitalist culture required a regimented and disciplined approach to work. There was a considerable struggle between workers and owners, as owners attempted to impose new work habits and a new way of life. Traditional rural pursuits and ways of life – the folk culture – were gradually suppressed by the culture of industrial and urban living. Gradually however, a new industrial working class was created, with a distinct set of cultural norms and values.

Richard Hoggart's book *The Uses of Literacy* provided a detailed description of the cultural norms and values of the working class which industrialisation created in the twentieth century. Hoggart's description of the working classes in the early twentieth century is of what sociologists would term the 'collectivistic' and 'solidaristic' traditional working class. The traditional working class were seen as being bound together by a strong community spirit, and an ethos of mutual support. For Hoggart, the cultural life of this class was also rich in terms of reading material, music, other leisure pursuits, and indeed, its whole way of life. Hoggart's view is that the cultural values created by modern society are inferior, and gradually they destroy the values and way of life of the traditional working class.

CLASS, CULTURE AND IDENTITY

The culture and identity of the working class has been the focus of considerable sociological interest, and views about working class culture have influenced sociological explanations in many topics, such as education, and crime and deviance. For many sociologists in the first half of the twentieth century, the working class were characterised in terms of what sociologists such as **Goldthorpe** and **Lockwood** termed the 'traditional working class'. The characteristics of this class included:

- work in a heavy industry, mining, metal work, and shipbuilding;
- culture (in terms of values and way of life) was solidaristic, present oriented;
- society was seen in terms of sharp social divisions between the rich and the poor;
- a keen sense of loyalty or solidarity; they cared for each other;
- a belief in the value of 'living for the moment', since there was no guarantee of what the future would bring. The future could for example, merely hold out the possibility of unemployment.

Such views of the traditional working class could be interpreted in varying ways, perhaps being seen by some as rather negative and stereotypical. Alternatively, in the case of Richard Hoggart's portrayal of the traditional working class during the early 1930s, it could well be argued that it is a rather romanticised view of the working class. The ways in which working class culture might be interpreted by other groups in society, and how the culture might influence the working class itself, can be demonstrated by considering sociologists' research on educational attainment in the 1960s.

- Consider whether and in what ways working class culture has changed in the late twentieth century. What factors are responsible for any changes identified?

CLASS AND CULTURAL DEPRIVATION

In contrast to the favourable picture of traditional working class culture provided by Thompson and Hoggart, sociologists in the 1960s argued that it was the cultural values of the working class which caused working class children to under-achieve in the education system. This was known as the 'cultural deprivation thesis'. The theory argued that the lower educational achievement of working class students could be explained in terms of the lower priority placed upon educational success by working class culture, which was present oriented, and valued instant gratification, rather than deferred gratification.

Research by sociologists such as **Herbert Hyman, Barry Sugarman**, and **J W B Douglas** appeared to support this theory. Sugarman for example suggested that the failure of working class students could be seen as a 'self-imposed barrier to success'. Douglas conducted a survey which aimed to measure parental interest by asking teachers which sorts of parents tended not to come to parents evenings. When teachers provided the information that working class parents were less frequently seen at parent evenings, Douglas reached the conclusion that such parents were clearly less committed to the educational success of their children.

Research on language by sociologists such as **Basil Bernstein** added a further dimension to the debate. Bernstein's work argued that working class students tended to use a 'restricted code' of language more frequently than 'elaborated codes', whereas the opposite was true of middle class students. Since the language of education and the middle classes is 'elaborated', working class students would clearly be at a disadvantage.

Other sociologists, such as **Halsey**, were later to put the case for alternative interpretations of this data. It was quite possible that economic factors, such as the need to work longer or unsocial hours, and the financial costs of travel, made attendance difficult for working class parents. Equally, cultural factors might work in a different way to that suggested by Douglas. It might be the case that working class parents were unconfident in their ability to deal adequately with the norms and values of schools and teachers. A Marxist interpretation would suggest that these values, of course, would be drawn in the main from the values of the dominant social classes. For critics of cultural deprivation theory it seemed that middle class sociologists were simply saying that working class culture was inferior. Whilst many sociologists would perhaps now agree that both cultural and economic factors contribute to educational attainment, these examples of research do seem to indicate that there are different class subcultures, and that when sociologists misunderstand these subcultures, their analyses can be inaccurate.

Study point

- Discuss whether there are cultural differences between the working class, the middle class, and the upper classes. Try to identify differences in values, way of life, and customs.

THE DECLINE OF CLASS IDENTITY?

More recently, sociologists such as **Peter Saunders** and **Ivor Crewe**, have argued that class is now of less importance to identity and political action.

Peter Saunders has argued that as Britain has become an increasingly wealthy society through the 1980s, social divisions other than class have become more important to people. Class, Saunders argues, is less important in terms of an individual's sense of identity than factors such as whether they own their own home or use private education or a private health care scheme. The political sociologist Ivor Crewe's analysis of voting behaviour in the mid and late 1980s shares some similarities with such a view. Crewe argued that voters were not making the same sort of broad class identification with the main political parties which they had made some 20 or 30 years previously. Crewe argued that the class alignment was declining, and that other factors, such as type of housing, sector of employment and the region where people lived, were becoming more important in determining voting behaviour.

Other research indicates that class can be an important source of identity in contemporary society. **Fiona Devine**, in her replication of the *Affluent Worker* study (published in 1992), found that many respondents did express a sense of belonging to a particular class, and as **Mark Kirby** has observed, the results of a Gallup opinion poll question asking whether respondents believed there was a class struggle in Britain in 1996, found 76% (and 81% in 1995) agreeing that there was a class struggle.

INTERPRETING THE EVIDENCE

Evidence on the importance of class to individual identity appears difficult to interpret. **Gordon Marshall's** research in the late 1980s indicated that whilst respondents (in a large sample) showed awareness of class position, there was no simple correlation with political views or anything which could be called a 'working class consciousness'. Fiona Devine concluded her study by arguing that class identity had to be seen in perspective as forming a part of people's identity, along with other factors such as regional and national identity. **Scott Lash** and **John Urry** have argued that whilst class remains a crucial aspect of social structure, and whilst contemporary society is still organised on capitalist principles, class can no longer be automatically assumed to be the key influence on individual identity. In taking such a stance, Devine, Lash and Urry reflect a growing view that, whilst class certainly is not dead, it is increasingly seen as only one of several structural factors in contemporary society. As **Harriet Bradley** has argued, contemporary sociologists tend to be interested in examining the complexities of the way in which class, ethnicity and gender are interrelated in society, rather than simply assuming the primacy of class. It would follow from these views that the importance of class culture has also changed; some would argue that it is consumer culture, not class culture which is of greater importance in contemporary society (see Chapter 9).

However, those who argue that class differences are no longer of any importance in contemporary society, can be seen as greatly exaggerating the importance of consumption and wealth. It can indeed be suggested that identities formed in terms of the ability to own a home, or to buy a private education, are simply reflections of class position, even if they are not thought of as such. Moreover, whilst there is evidence of considerable wealth in societies like Britain, this relates to particular types of wealth. There are for instance, high levels of ownership for consumer goods such as telephones, 'white' and 'black' goods and cars. There are high levels of home ownership. However, these figures have to be interpreted in the context of conclusive evidence, based upon the government's own figures showing a widening of the income gap between the richest and poorest.

Whilst class remains of importance then, the class structure, and the nature of class culture, certainly is changing. People are living more individualised lifestyles, and may be open to a much wider range of influences and experiences than previous generations of their family. However, if the traditional working class community identified by writers such as Richard Hoggart is now largely gone, it does not mean that class culture is no longer used as a way of identifying, placing and judging individuals and social groups. This can be illustrated by examining the recent debates on the existence of an 'underclass' and the so-called 'dependency culture'.

DEPENDENCY CULTURE AND THE UNDERCLASS

In recent years there has been increasing use of the terms 'underclass', and 'dependency culture'. Both terms have led to considerable sociological debate. Perhaps the most well known exponent of the concept of underclass and dependency culture has been the American sociologist **Charles Murray**.

The identification of distinct strata within the working class is not a new phenomenon. Sociologists have noted distinctions being made between the so-called 'rough' and 'respectable' sections of the working class for a long time. It has also been observed that these distinctions are essentially being made not so much upon the basis of economic criteria, but on grounds of the values and way of life of sections of the working class. This has frequently led to criticism of the use of such terms, since it has been argued that they say more about the researcher's own values and attitudes, than about the structure of the working class.

Charles Murray came to prominence with the publication of an article in *The Sunday Times* magazine in 1988, arguing that an urban underclass, which already existed in the USA, was developing in Britain. The underclass had many characteristics, and consisted of a variety of different sorts of people. Murray included in the underclass the long term unemployed, young single parents and drug addicts. Murray noted also the prevalence of black males in such a group, and the high rate of crime which went along with inner-city areas populated by such people. Since Murray's article was published, further commentators have suggested other groups who may belong to the underclass, including the elderly, the homeless and new age travellers. Murray argued that the underclass was the result of an over-generous welfare state, which provided benefits too easily, and gave little incentive for people to go and find work. He thus argued that the underclass had what he termed a 'dependency culture'. Murray argued that those in the underclass had developed a distinct set of values. They would not for instance have a work ethic, nor a strong belief in family values, nor necessarily show much respect for the rules and laws of mainstream society. They had become dependent on welfare benefits.

One critic of such views is the British sociologist **Lydia Morris**. In her book, *The Dangerous Classes*, Morris notes that the practice of scapegoating the poorest members of society, and perceiving them as a threat to the wider society, has a long history which reflects the fears and concerns of capitalist culture. Morris argues that the use of the term underclass has become common as a result of changes in the labour market, affecting in particular those at the bottom of the class structure. The globalisation of capitalism has led firms to cut down on their labour force and attempt to reduce costs. This has in turn led to high male unemployment and an increase in poorly paid part-time work for women, whilst at the same time there has been an increase in single parent families (usually female headed). It is these trends which have led to the existence of what some term 'the underclass'.

Morris concludes that the concept of underclass is helpful to portray the way in which individuals with a certain status – unemployed, single parent and so on, are excluded from full membership of society, and seen as outcasts by the majority. This analysis thus suggests that it is the culture of the wider society which defines and describes an underclass as a stigmatised group. How the functions of such cultural exclusion and stigmatised identity are interpreted, will depend upon the sociological perspective taken by the observer.

MODERN SOCIETY AND MASS CULTURE

Other sociologists have been interested in examining the ways in which industrial societies create cultural products, such as music, art, literature and the mass media. These sociologists have been interested in the effects of these products, the way in which they are produced, and the shared meanings which they may demonstrate. A particular interest for many sociologists has been the area of popular culture (or mass culture), which sociologists have been keen to analyse for insights into the cultural values and beliefs of contemporary society.

The Frankfurt School Marxists (see Chapter 4), have seen modern capitalist society as leading to the creation of a mass or popular culture. **Walter Benjamin**, a member of the Frankfurt School, argued that once industrial society had created the means of mass production, it simply applied the same principles to cultural products. This meant that artistic endeavour and its products could be mass produced. Whilst the works of artists such as Cézanne, or Leonardo da Vinci, would previously have been on show only in art galleries, industrial technology meant that not only could they be viewed by a mass audience on television or in books, but everyone could have their own print!

Modern society has also seen what some sociologists have termed the 'differentiation of the cultural sphere'. In modern society, in contrast to traditional society, cultural activity has become seen as something worthwhile and important for its own sake, and as a specialised activity. Moreover, unlike previous periods in history, where art may have been used for religious or social purposes, in modernity, art serves no purpose except to be artistic. The Frankfurt School and others would point out that the twentieth century has seen the development of the 'culture industry'; those employed in the arts, publishing, films, television and the media. For the Frankfurt School, this meant that art and culture in the twentieth century became mass produced, inevitably lowering the quality of artistic and cultural production.

CONTRASTING DRESS FOR 'HIGH' CULTURE ...

...AND 'POPULAR' CULTURE

These observations on the nature of culture in capitalist society have led to considerable interest and debate amongst Marxist sociologists and other commentators, about the role of popular culture in contemporary society. Some Marxists have focused upon the issues involved in the production of culture, and particular on issues such as ownership and control of the media and cultural producers. Others, influenced by Gramsci (neo-Marxists), have examined popular culture as a form of resistance to the dominant class culture. The Frankfurt School, as previously noted, have examined popular culture as a form of social control, providing an ideological support for capitalism.

These different views within Marxism have led to the development of what is often called the 'popular culture debate'. Essentially the debate is over how popular culture should be interpreted by sociologists. Also at issue have been related questions as to how cultural categories are constructed, used and reproduced. Sociologists have usually examined these issues in terms of the way in which culture is both produced and consumed in a class dividied society.

Study point

- Give examples of the cultural values reflected in soap operas such as Eastenders. Do these programmes reproduce the dominant cultural norms and values of our society? Consider issues of gender differences, ethnicity, age, sexuality and attitudes to crime and violence.

THE PRODUCTION AND CONSUMPTION OF CULTURE

The issue of how sociologists' own values may influence research into culture has been discussed at several previous points in this book. The issue of values makes the study of culture in terms of artistic and creative activities particularly problematic, and sociological accounts may often be found to be implying, implicitly or explicitly, that one level of culture is better than another.

These problems are particularly apparent in the popular culture debate. In other cases, the problem faced by many Marxist accounts is one of economic reductionism. This section will draw upon and develop several of the concepts and approaches discussed in Chapter 4, and will suggest that understanding the social function of the various levels of culture requires a consideration of structure and action approaches, and economic and cultural factors.

Golding and Murdock exemplify the Marxist political economy approach, which has been particularly open to the criticism of being economically reductionist. Whilst it may be readily accepted that cultural production is importantly influenced by the ownership and control of the culture industries, it can be argued that it is not simply economic factors which determine cultural production, and power is not always successfully monopolised by the capitalist class. A good example of these points is provided by sociologist **Keith Negus'** study of the singer George Michael's dispute with his recording company, Sony.

GEORGE MICHAEL AND CULTURAL AUTONOMY

As Negus recounts, George Michael's problems started soon after Sony bought out CBS, to whom Michael was contracted, in the late 1980s. This happened to coincide with a period of uncertainty for Michael over the way in which his career was developing. It seems that Michael was concerned to effect a change in his image; as he was becoming older, he was aware that his audience and their tastes would also change. Michael became increasingly unhappy with Sony when sales for his albums dropped, feeling that Sony were not doing enough to promote and market them. Michael, according to press reports, felt that this was part of an attempt by Sony to force him to go back to his previous 'pop' image; whereas he was attempting to gain the image of 'serious adult artist'. To this end his first album for Sony carried no picture of him, and was promoted with an in-depth interview on the serious arts programme, *The Southbank Show*. After a series of failed negotiations, Michael's dispute ended in court, with Michael attempting to obtain a release from his contract with Sony.

Michael lost his case against Sony and, since he could not legally work for anyone else, vowed never to record again. The dispute was finally resolved in 1993 when after lengthy discussions and complex legal and financial agreements, Michael signed for Virgin and another company. The point Negus makes about the case, is that it shows that the giant corporation of Sony was not able to get its way, and mould Michael into a compliant puppet who would produce whatever was demanded. Negus argues that this indicates that the political economy view of cultural production can be far too simplistic. Negus suggests that it is not simply economic considerations which drive cultural production, but also ideas of taste; the differences between the two parties were not simply financial, they were about artistic issues. The study also shows that individual cultural producers can pressurise the large cultural corporations.

YOUTH CULTURE AS RESISTANCE

Neo-Marxist approaches to cultural production have applied the ideas of Gramsci to popular culture. Gramsci's work focused upon the way in which capitalism was legitimated by the process of ideological hegemony. However, Gramsci noted that hegemony was always the result of resistance and opposition. Gramsci's theories were particularly influential upon the academics based at the Centre for Contemporary Cultural Studies (CCCS) at Birmingham University. Many of these researchers were also influenced by semiotics – the study of signs and symbolism – and they attempted to synthesise an interpretation of the cultural symbols, such as style, clothes and music, of youth subcultures, with analysis of the class origins of these cultural forms.

Skinhead subculture

One example is **John Clarke**'s analysis of the meaning of skinhead subcultural style in the 1960s and 1970s. Clarke argued that the clothes worn by skinheads represented an exaggerated and stylised version of traditional working class style. Doc Marten boots, braces and extremely short haircuts had the effect of symbolising both where these people were from, and what sort of people they were. Skinhead style reflected the fears of traditional working class culture in the face of economic decline and immigration, although this is not to claim that skinheads were necessarily conscious of such an interpretation. The clothes and the style, however, denoted a tough, independent identity.

Punk rock

Dick Hebdige's study, *Subculture – The Meaning of Style*, is another example, examining a number of youth subcultures, but with a particular focus on the punk movement of the late 1970s. Hebdige argues that punk rock can be understood as a form of resistance to the dominant cultural values of British society in the late 1970s. This was a society in economic and cultural decline, which arguably had little to offer working class youth, particularly given high levels of youth unemployment.

Hebdige explains that the symbolism and style of punk rock, such as safety pins stuck in the nose, blank stares and 'pogo' dancing for example, reflected deep cultural resistances to the dominant culture. These symbols represented an inverting of common norms and values. Rather than trying to look attractive, and indeed to look like interested participants in society, punks went out of their way to look ugly and to shock. In essence, by adopting such a style, punk rockers were signifying that if they did live in an ugly, oppressive and declining country, then they would act accordingly.

For Hebdige, punks were trying to escape from the identities on offer to them, and which they would be labelled with. Hebdige argues that subcultures operate by identifying contradictions in the dominant culture and then subverting them. Thus the punks identified the contradictions and hypocrisy of the turgid 'rock establishment' of the 1970s, which masqueraded as providing artistic freedom but was (in their view) in reality controlled by the giant American music corporations. Punks subverted this by producing deliberately badly played music and offensive and garish record sleeves, and giving themselves unattractive names, such as Johnny Rotten, Sid Vicious, Rat Scabies, Richard Hell and Poly Styrene. The anarchic, chaotic and subversive spirit of the music is reflected in the titles of the Sex Pistols songs, 'Anarchy in the UK', and 'God Save the Queen (the fascist regime)', and their album title *Never mind the Bollocks*.

As Hebdige points out, subcultures in capitalist society, whilst they legitimate the cultural hegemony by their existence, are sooner or later incorporated into the dominant culture. This occurs in two ways. Firstly, the elements of the subculture are commodified (see Chapter 4), and turned into consumer objects, despite the intentions of the subculture members. Thus, bands such as the Sex Pistols and The Clash got recording contracts, made lots of money, and were then required by their contract to make further records. Punk clothes were manufactured by fashion companies and quickly increased in price. Secondly, punk was ideologically labelled and redefined. Punk came to be labelled as exotic and spirited, perhaps even funny, but also quite harmless. Pictures of punks with unusual haircuts became the sort of thing put on postcards or school textbooks.

Study point

- Suggest alternative interpretations of punk subculture to those offered by Hebdige. Consider the difficulties in evaluating the validity of Hebdige's interpretation.

Activity

Examine several contemporary youth cultures, using perhaps a small number of semi-structured interviews. Attempt to assess to what extent their values are different to that of the wider society. Consider what functions the subculture fulfils, and whether it reflects the social status or class position of any particular group.

THE FRANKFURT SCHOOL – CONDESCENDING ELITISTS?

Several key criticisms have been made of the Frankfurt School's critical theory in terms of it's applications to an understanding of cultural production. It has been seen as elitist (see Chapter 4), to assume a passive view of the audience, to be blind to its own value assumptions, and to neglect the variety of popular culture. In addition many critics have seen it, in common with all Marxist based theories, as viewing culture as the result of economic processes; as an economically deterministic theory (see for instance, Strinati 1993).

Critics such as **Strinati** would argue that cultural production is not solely determined by the economic structure of society, and stress the need to see the role of ideas and beliefs as distinct and autonomous. To paraphrase Strinati, culture is not always related to the class struggle. Neither should cultural production – the making of cultural artefacts such as television, film, books, art – be seen as simply serving an ideological purpose, and as acting as a mechanism of social control. Indeed, art and culture may frequently be used as the basis for social and political criticism. A key task for the sociological study of popular culture is to consider how culture is experienced and interpreted by people, rather than just assuming that people will react or be influenced in a certain way.

EVALUATION – THE PRODUCTION AND CONSUMPTION
OF POPULAR CULTURE

Marxist views, which have made a great contribution to studying popular culture, have tended to have several faults. Either, they have been economically reductionist, and seen all popular culture as a reflection of the class structure, or they have been elitist and seen popular culture as a poor relation to 'proper' culture. Both of these problems have meant that Marxist analysis of popular culture may be lacking, particularly if the aim is to investigate the meaning which popular culture has for individuals and society.

Whilst sociologists such as Strinati can criticise the Frankfurt School for their elitism, others, such as **Jim McGuigan**, have accused the CCCS tradition of 'cultural populism'; assuming that all popular culture is both good and a resistance to a dominant class culture. What is needed is a more flexible view, which acknowledges the way in which social actors actively construct cultural categories whilst situated within the structural constraints of a class system.

CULTURAL CONSUMPTION AND CULTURAL CAPITAL

A key contribution to understanding cultural consumption has been made by the French sociologist **Pierre Bourdieu**. Bourdieu is interested in the cultural aspects of class, and his analysis points out that judgements about culture reflect the class structure of society. One of Bourdieu's key concepts is that of 'habitus'. By this term, Bourdieu simply wishes to refer to the key principles, values and behavioural norms which a particular class or social group uphold. Classes inevitably compete with each other for status, but Bourdieu points out that members of classes do not just have differing amounts of economic resources – or capital, they also have varying amounts of cultural capital. By cultural capital, Bourdieu refers to the values and norms which members of different classes will uphold, and which provide them with status. Consumption or, more simply, spending, is one way in which this can be achieved. Thus members of different social classes, but with fairly similar incomes, will make different choices in terms of the sort of music they enjoy, what they watch on television, or the sort of theatre performance they enjoy. There are for instance strong class differences in the audiences for classical music and country and western music. Television stations such as BBC2, Channel 4, and Sky, will also have class biases in their audience, with BBC2 and Channel 4 viewers tending to be drawn from higher socio-economic classes than say Sky or ITV. Equally, so-called 'serious' theatre, such as performances by the Royal Shakespeare Company or the National Theatre, has a different audience to popular West End musicals. These are differences between high culture and popular culture. For Bourdieu, the differing status which accrues to each is representative, not of their intrinsic merit, but rather their position in a class-based value scheme. Which of these forms of culture has greater artistic merit or aesthetic value is not an issue which sociologists are particularly qualified to answer.

WATCHING *DALLAS* – POPULAR CULTURE AND THE CRITICAL AUDIENCE

A more flexible approach to popular culture, which acknowledges the audiences' ability to interpret and yet also recognises important structural constraints, is demonstrated by **Ien Ang**'s study, *Watching Dallas*. Ang conducted a study during the 1980s into audience response to the American soap opera *Dallas*. Ang placed an advert in a newspaper, asking for women to write in with their views on the programme, and received 39 responses which were then analysed. Ang argued that women responded to popular culture in several ways, and were not simply to be seen as duped by it. Those viewers who claimed to dislike the programme and mocked it, were more confident in their assessment, compared to those who claimed that they really did enjoy it, who were rather reticent in defending their choice. Ang suggests that the reason for this is that the first set of viewers drew upon a view of mass culture, rather like that of the Frankfurt School, which simply categorised *Dallas* as a cheap and simplistic product of mass culture. The other set of viewers were guided by an alternative ideology, one of populism. Ang characterises this view as implying that if a cultural product is popular, then it should be tolerated. Ang's findings suggest that while audiences can respond to popular culture in a variety of ways, cultural tastes are influenced by ideologies which audiences may have differential access to. The ideologies which influence an individual will be related to their class position.

Activity

Make a list of television programmes, music, films and other cultural forms, and attempt to create a chart indicating the cultural preferences of different social classes. Use a questionnaire survey to see if this chart is reflected in reality. Attempt to discover if there are different judgements of popular culture according to class. Do for instance, middle class and working class viewers of *Eastenders*, have different attitudes to the programme?

CULTURAL CAPITAL, EDUCATION AND ELITES

Bourdieu's concepts can also be applied to examine other aspects of culture. They have been applied in the sociology of education, where the concept of cultural capital has been used to explain differences in attainment. The concept of habitus implies that different social classes have different principles and behave in different ways. Since schools are institutions largely designed and run by the middle classes, the value systems they represent are not simply alien to those from other class backgrounds; they also act to reproduce status differences between the different social classes.

Bourdieu's analysis suggests that working class failure is the result, not of a poorer culture or a lack of interest on the part of working class students, but simply their lack of cultural capital. So for example, working class students may enjoy reading, but more popular reading material is frequently not encouraged in an education system which requires students to be familiar with Shakespeare or Dickens. The reading material favoured by working class children may even be actively criticised by schools and educational authorities. In the case of art, working class students may be keen 'graffiti artists'; schools and other authorities would not consider this to be art, nor would work in this genre be encouraged. Music provides another good example of an area of 'culture clash', where the abilities and talents of those from a different culture will find their activity negatively labelled. Middle class students on the other hand, are consistently advantaged in the education system, since their cultural principles and values are continually being used in schools. They find that educational activities, and the language, norms and values, of the school system, match their own culture and value system. This invariably provides them with an advantage, since they will rarely feel culturally out of place. The education system can be seen as simply reproducing the culture of the dominant classes.

Cultural capital and habitus can also apply to the minute details of social behaviour. There are for instance, a variety of eating and drinking habits amongst different social classes. For those unused to formal dining, an array of knives, forks, spoons, and different glasses for particular drinks, can create a formidable social occasion likely to cause embarrassment and confusion.

These may seem minor issues, but **John Scott**'s research on the upper classes shows the importance of knowing the right ways to behave to gain positions in the top echelons of British society. Those at the top of British society tend to originate from a restricted group of elite circles, and common educational experience at top public schools and Oxford and Cambridge universities teaches successive generations of the elite how to behave in the right way. As Scott notes, it is for this reason that the socially ambitious are keen to secure entry to the public schools and the elite universities for their children. The social etiquette, and the connections (networking) which such young people make, being as, if not more, important than the academic content of their degree courses.

SUMMARY

Modernist sociology has been centrally concerned with class. Tastes are influenced by class. It has also been observed that some sociologists have argued that class is of less importance in contemporary society. Whilst it has been suggested that this view is exaggerated, it raises important issues. Many sociologists have suggested that the biases of modernist sociology, some of which have been apparent in this chapter, are not simply confined to the issue of class. Gender and ethnicity are also important aspects of contemporary culture and society, and key aspects of identity. These topics are considered in the following chapters.

Group Work

1 Conduct research to investigate the influence of occupational class on identity. How does a person's job affect their identity?
2 Debate the motions 'True style and taste is always set by an elite' and 'The working class are culturally deprived'.
3 Apply Marxist theories to examine the social significance of rap music. Use CD-Rom to access the articles by Playthell Benjamin in *The Guardian* 11th March and 25th January, 1993 (use author/byline search).

Practice questions

ITEM A

According to the Frankfurt School, the culture industry reflects the consolidation of commodity fetishism, the domination of exchange value and the ascendancy of state monopoly capitalism. It shapes the tastes and preferences of the masses, thereby moulding their consciousness by inculcating a desire for false needs. It therefore works to exclude real or true needs, alternative and radical concepts or theories, and politically oppositional ways of thinking and acting. It is so effective in doing this that the people do not realise what is going on.

Dominic Strinati, An Introduction to Theories of Popular Culture, Routledge, 1995, p61

ITEM B

The Marxist view of class culture is that socio-economic factors lead to different classes having different patterns of meaning, therefore it is questioned whether an overall shared culture exists in society. Class culture arises out of shared interests. Others disagree, and argue that there is a dominant culture which all members of society broadly share, irrespective of differences which may arise from other characteristics such as age, class, or ethnic group.

Lawson and Garrod, A–Z Sociology Handbook, Hodder & Stoughton, 1996, p55

1 Briefly explain what is meant by the term 'commodity fetishism' (Item A). (3)
2 Give three criticisms of the view expressed in Item A.   (3)
3 With reference to the concept of cultural capital, suggest two examples of the ways in which dominant classes are able to define their own culture as superior, and establish it as the basis for knowledge in the education system.   (3)
4 Critically assess the usefulness of the Frankfurt School's approach to popular culture (Item A) .   (8)
5 Using material in the Items and elsewhere, critically evaluate the view that different classes have different patterns of meaning.   (8)

Coursework

1 Conduct research to investigate the importance of cultural factors in explaining differences in educational attainment.
2 Test the hypothesis that cultural consumption will vary according to social class, focusing on either reading matter (novels, or newspapers) or television viewing.
3 Test the theory that there is a 'dependency culture', a distinct set of norms and values held by the unemployed or the homeless. You could gain access to these groups of people through welfare agencies, charitable organisations, or newspapers like *The Big Issue*.

7

GENDER, AGE AND THE BODY

Introduction

Table 6: *Theorists, concepts and issues in this chapter*		
KEY THEORISTS	KEY CONCEPTS	KEY ISSUES
• Sylvia Walby & Carole Pateman • Janet Woolf • Ann Oakley • Michelle Stanworth • Jean Duncombe & Dennis Marsden • Anthony King • Joyce Canaan • Mairtin Mac an Ghaill • Andrea Dworkin & Catherine MacKinnon • Tom Shakespeare • Jennifer Hockey & Allison James	Patriarchy Patriarchal culture Malestream society Public and private spheres Emotional work Sociology of the body Infantilisation	How is gender constructed by culture, and are there significant differences in the range of identities open to men and women? How are views about the human body influenced by culture, and how do people use their body as a resource to create particular identities? How is age treated in western culture, and how does this influence the construction of identity?

THIS CHAPTER EXAMINES the way in which feminism has led sociologists to consider the ways in which identity and gender are socially constructed, and to see that gender differences are best understood as cultural rather than natural forms of behaviour which we learn through socialisation. Feminism has also led sociologists more recently to consider issues such as the role of masculinity and age in the construction of identity, and the way in which people may use their body as a resource for creating a particular identity.

MODERNITY AND MALESTREAM SOCIOLOGY

Until fairly recently it would have been possible for sociologists to refer to Marx, Durkheim and Weber as the 'founding fathers' of the discipline, without attracting any criticism whatsoever. Over the past 30 years or so, feminist sociologists have argued that modernist sociology has, from its beginnings, been a biased project. Feminists have described modernist sociology as 'patriarchal', that is they have seen it as a sociology made from and reflecting (perhaps unintentionally) a male dominated perspective of society. For feminist sociologists mainstream academic sociology has neglected or misrepresented the role and experience of women in modern society. **Ann Oakley** for instance, wrote her ground breaking book, *Housewife*, in order to make the point that housework was indeed work, albeit unpaid work. She felt that analyses of work in capitalist society by male sociologists had entirely ignored an important area of sociological enquiry. Such views were shared by many young women embarking upon academic careers, and feminist approaches gained great popularity. Much later on, feminist sociologists **Pamela Abbott** and **Claire Wallace**, in a deliberate play on words, referred to mainstream academic sociology as 'malestream sociology'. The term stuck, and is now widely used by sociologists, both male and female.

THE SOCIOLOGY OF THE BODY

There has thus been an increasing interest in gender issues amongst sociologists. Whilst this started with a focus on women's issues, it has now broadened to include the study of masculinity, and these concerns in turn have led sociologists to focus on issues such as physical appearance and age. These interests have led to the development of a new area of sociological study, the sociology of the body. As a result new issues previously rather neglected in sociology, such as sexuality and disability, have come onto the sociological agenda.

The study of such intimate and apparently natural aspects of our lives – our sexuality, our body and the ageing process, are aspects which many people would feel are most closely tied to nature. Sociology, they might reason, can tell us little about these areas, and we must look instead to biology or sociobiology. However, the sociological approach suggests otherwise. Sex, body and age, whilst all relating to nature and natural processes, are also aspects of life which are socially organised. Our individual identity, and our feelings about it, is a result of the cultural norms and values which we learn about sex, body and age.

FEMINISM, PATRIARCHY AND MODERNITY

Modern industrial society has been characterised by a patriarchal culture which has structured the identities and lifechances of both men and women.

Feminist sociologists have provided a number of ways of explaining the patriarchal culture of modern societies. **Sherry Ortner** has argued that all cultures place women in a subordinate position because femininity is somehow seen as 'closer to nature'. Ortner argues that the biological facts of womens lives, such as pregnancy, childcare, menstruation and lactation, are interpreted as evidence that women are more closely tied to nature than men. This leads to women's role being devalued. The view that women are more emotional and less logical than men, and that biological characteristics make women substantially different from men, both psychologically and physically, would be logical extensions of this idea.

Study point

- Suggest three criticisms of the biological view that women are more emotional and less logical than men.

WOMEN IN THE PUBLIC AND PRIVATE SPHERES

Other sociologists, such as **Sylvia Walby** and **Carole Pateman**, would argue that patriarchy in modern societies is distinctive. Drawing on structural theories, Walby and Pateman point out that modern industrial societies have seen the creation of two distinct spheres of social activity, the public and the private. The public sphere simply refers to those aspects of our lives which are conducted in public: education, work, and the ways in which these things are organised by political systems. The private sphere in contrast, refers to the areas of our lives which, although very much influenced by society, are conducted in private: our family and home lives, and sexuality. In pre-industrial societies it can be argued, these distinctions did not exist in the same way, since life was lived in smaller communities, and distinctions between home and work, work and leisure, and public and private were less evident.

Industrialisation led to the progressive exclusion of women from the public sphere. Legislation was passed throughout the nineteenth century prohibiting and regulating women's ability to work, and the development of the welfare state embodied patriarchal views on the rightful place of women in the family, looking after their husband and children.

Janet Woolf has shown how the culture of modern society, and the creation of public and private spheres, has influenced the identities open to men and women. Borrowing a phrase from the sociologist **Richard Sennett**, Woolf refers to the way that modern industrial society led to the 'privatisation of personality', indicating the way in which industrialisation and urbanisation led to a society which enabled individuals to define their own identity, rather than having it defined for them by a small and close knit community.

As Woolf points out however, this was not something which worked in the same way for all groups in society. In many ways women were confined to the private sphere, and excluded from many public activities and places. Thus in the eighteenth and nineteenth century, there were very strict rules governing where women could be seen and who they could speak to. Cafés, pubs and gentlemen's clubs were generally out of bounds. In order to enable others to distinguish the 'respectable lady' from the 'loose woman', women had to take particular care over their dress and other signs of social status. These cultural norms are so strong that despite considerable social change, women's use of public space, such as bars and clubs, is still open to critical comment and interpretation from men. Janet Woolf points out that the confinement of women to the private spheres of life, was of course, not a complete one. Women continued to work throughout the nineteenth century, for instance, and were not hidden from sight.

Activity

Undertake a short piece of research by questionnaire or face to face interview with a sample of people of different ages to find out if there are any clubs, pubs or cafés in the area which you live or study which women would not enter alone. What explanations are given and is there any reason to suggest that they are correct in their feelings?

However, the ways in which women appeared in the public sphere developed in a particular way. Woolf notes that it was in the 1850s and 60s that the department store was established. As urban centres grew, so too did consumer facilities. Whilst women were not completely excluded from the public sphere, their place within it was often seen in terms of their roles in the private sphere. Thus, for women, shopping was not just a form of public activity which was permissable, it was an essential part of the female role and identity in modern urban society. Arguably it is from these historical origins that we can trace current issues including women's fear of being *alone* in urban areas, and the stigmatising of unattached single females in public places.

Patriarchal culture though, is not simply something which affects women. It has a variety of influences upon both male and female identity, and it is now necessary to examine these in more detail.

PATRIARCHY, CULTURE AND IDENTITY

The influence of patriarchy upon identity was something first mapped out by feminist sociologists, such as Ann Oakley, **Sue Sharpe**, and **Sue Lees**. Oakley argued that girls were subjected to subtle pressures from the earliest stages of socialisation, by having their activities channelled and directed. Sharpe and Lees, amongst others, conducted the empirical research which provided the evidence for these claims. Sue Sharpe's study of a group of schoolgirls in a London comprehensive school showed how their ambitions and sense of identity were centred around the goals of marriage and children. Sue Lees' study illustrated that the gender socialisation of girls was influenced by the social control exerted by young males, reinforced by the patriarchal culture of the wider society. Lees' study indicated how 'reputational labelling' adversely affected girls, and how a considerable part of their behaviour centred around avoiding a negative label. Lees revealed how young boys use terms such as 'slag', 'tart' and 'bitch' to label females. Such labelling acted as a form of social control, discouraging (sanctioning) girls who attempted to challenge popular and dominant notions of femininity. Girls attracting such negative labels were often not promiscuous at all, but simply departed from the commonly expected forms of behaviour for young females, by for example, swearing, spitting or using violence.

GENDERING IDENTITY – EDUCATION AND WORK

Research by other sociologists has indicated the ways in which patriarchal culture continues to influence women's identity in education, work, and marriage. **Michelle Stanworth**'s study of gender and schooling showed how gender socialisation was reinforced by schools and teachers, who held stereotyped views of girls' abilities and aptitudes. Stanworth found that many teachers felt that girls were not interested in careers; it was believed that their real interests were in boys, marriage and having children. Such views are reinforced by the dominant values of patriarchal society – that a career is of lesser importance for women, that girls are suited to particular types of work – and the prevalence of sexist attitudes in many work places. The lower priority placed upon a woman's career is amply illustrated by Sharpe, Stanworth and Lees' research.

Whilst attitudes are changing, stereotyped views as to women's aptitudes persist, as is indicated by the types of work in which women tend to find employment. In terms of manual labour, women are frequently found in light assembly work, since the common view is that women are good at tasks requiring dexterity. **Anna Pollert** found this to be the case in her study of work in a cigarette factory. It is also reflected in the large proportion of women working in other light assembly work, in the electronics industry for example. **Rosemary Crompton** has shown that the representation of women in the professions is improving, but still women are more heavily represented in fields which are seen to be in some way more feminine.

Similarly women working in business will tend to be found more frequently in personnel, that is involved in the 'soft' emotional aspects of business in contrast to the hard world of manufacturing. In medicine women tend to be concentrated in specialisms dealing with childcare, or in the less prestigious specialisms generally, whilst in the legal profession family law contains a high proportion of women.

Study point
• What is meant by the 'glass ceiling' which is sometimes said to restrict women's work opportunities? Suggest some reasons why women continue to be under-represented in most professions, especially at the highest levels.

PATRIARCHY, IDENTITY AND THE EMOTIONS

As has been indicated, feminists have argued that industrial society created the distinction between public and private spheres, with important results for patriarchal culture and women's identity. Feminists have suggested that patriarchal culture has tended to portray women as closer to nature than men, and thus more at the mercy of nature. This can lead to women and femininity being seen as irrational, more emotional, and more tied to the constraints of biological functions. Such characteristics in patriarchal culture can be seen as providing an explanation and justification for the restriction of women's activities to the public sphere.

Research conducted by **Jean Duncombe** and **Dennis Marsden** provides a good illustration of the ways in which patriarchal culture influences women's everyday lives. Duncombe and Marsden note that much sociological research into gender relations and conjugal roles has had an instrumental or economic focus, asking questions about how much time men spend doing housework or childcare, or finding out how husbands and wives control household finances. Sociologists have tended to neglect investigating emotions and intimacy, perhaps seeing these as the territory of psychologists and other disciplines. In the light of the 'new man' phenomenon, Duncombe and Marsden argue that their research indicates that men still show great reluctance to display emotional feelings, and that this is a cultural, not a natural phenomenon. Patriarchal culture it is argued, creates a socially constructed division which portrays men as rational and women as emotional.

Emotion work

Duncombe and Marsden point out that it was the functionalist sociologist Talcott Parsons who first described male and female roles as non-affective and affective (emotional), and saw the social roots of such roles as lying in the process of socialisation, not in biological differences between the sexes. Drawing on the work of American sociologist **Arlie Hochschild**, Duncombe and Marsden argue that women become skilled in displaying and using emotions from a very early age. Arlie Hochschild suggests that women tend to put more effort than men into what she terms 'emotion work'. By this, Hochschild means the way in which we control our emotions in terms of expectations about how we should expect to feel in certain situations. Hochschild gives the example of the way in which many married women put on an act of 'happiness', or 'play the happy families game', even though they may in reality be unhappy about their husband's lack of involvement in everyday family life.

Duncombe and Marsden's own research, conducted on a sample of 40 couples who had been married for 15 years, indicated that Hochschild's views were accurate. It was found that men gave priority to their work, were frequently psychologically and sometimes physically absent from the marriage, and if engaged in a task like childminding, would do something else at the same time. This last point illustrates men's comparative remoteness from the family. Women were more likely to devote all their attention to the task, and less likely to see it as a chore. Emotion work changes as a marriage progresses, indeed it may become harder as disillusionment sets in. As Duncombe and Marsden put it, there is 'gender asymmetry in emotional behaviour', and this is the result of cultural, rather than biological constraints on behaviour.

PATRIARCHAL CULTURE AND MASCULINE IDENTITY

The previous sections have mainly focused on the effects of patriarchal culture on female identity. However, it is important to appreciate that patriarchal culture also affects men. Malestream sociology has been slow to reflect upon this aspect of gender studies but there is now increasing interest in the sociological study of masculinity. **Paul Willis**'s study, *Learning to Labour*, whilst focusing on explaining working class education underachievement, raised many issues about the study of gender. Willis studied a small group of male students, whose cultural identity was centrally formed by rejecting the values of the school. In contrast the boys sought after what they saw as the adult and masculine freedoms of manual labour. This was a world in which values of toughness, strength, aggression and independence were recognised and valued. The boys derided the values of the school, which they felt were effeminate. Academic work was seen as exhibiting what they saw as feminine characteristics. Teachers and conformist pupils were generally seen by the boys as weak and incapable of doing really demanding tasks, such as physical work.

More recent research confirms aspects of Willis's work. **Anthony King** has used participant observation and informal interviews with a small group of football fans to investigate the effect of changes in the way football is marketed and consumed as a product. King has been particularly interested in how such changes may affect the self-concept and sense of masculinity of those whom he sees as 'traditional' fans. In fact, King terms the fans he investigates 'the lads', the same term used by Willis to describe his respondents.

King found that 'the lads' were unhappy with many aspects of the recent commercialisation of football, particularly those which changed their traditional forms of behaviour at matches. King explains this by arguing that going to football matches is an important aspect of traditional working class male identity. Supporting a football team provides a young man with a sense of identity and status. It is also a way of proving that one holds certain key male attributes, such as loyalty, demonstrated through regular attendance and indeed, a willingness to fight for one's club. A vital part of the whole process for 'the lads' was being able to stand up, sing, chant, sway and drink with their mates. New all-seater stadiums have made this difficult, if not impossible, and thus 'the lads' and supporters like them are disenchanted with many of the changes made. This research raises the question of how masculinity is changing and being changed by consumer society (see Chapter 8).

PATRIARCHY, MASCULINITY AND VIOLENCE

Joyce Canaan's research on young working class men provides further indications of the nature of contemporary masculinity, as well as attempting to examine how it is changing. Canaan conducted ethnographic research in Wolverhampton, using a variety of methods including informal interviews, and examining differences between the employed and the unemployed. Canaan found that drinking, fighting, and male sexuality were key elements of masculine identity for young working class men. A central part of their identity, and a good deal of their daily activity, centred around proving and maintaining a reputation for being 'hard'. Indeed, young men were even able to map out their town in terms of 'hard' and 'soft' areas. Canaan argues that these young men had shifted their emotions from a psychological level to a physical level. Drinking was seen as a necessary part of fighting, since it allowed them to loose self-control and bring out an aspect of their identity which was normally hidden. It could also be a way of proving masculinity, either through one's capacity to 'hold' drink, or through the display of outrageous behaviour which a man might indulge in when drunk. The men's protective attitude towards women, reflected their belief that women needed the protection of a man, but crucially, it also enabled them to put the woman in the position of being a subordinate or dependent.

Canaan found that the experience of unemployed men was rather different. They were deprived of the key status symbol of masculinity, the label 'breadwinner'. It seems that many men felt this to be an almost emasculating process. Unsurprisingly perhaps, such men tended to be much less concerned with drinking and fighting.

Mairtin Mac an Ghaill has argued that the increase in male unemployment and the increase in female semi-skilled employment, has led to a form of identity crisis for many working class men. Mac an Ghaill argues that with the loss of the ability to earn, and in many cases the need to become dependent upon a woman, such working class men are unable to gain status in the traditional ways; through being a wage-earner, drinking with male friends, and so on.

VARIATIONS IN MASCULINITIES

The sociologist **Robert Connell** has argued that sociologists need to examine masculinities, rather than assume that there is only one version of masculinity. Connell adopts a Gramscian (see Chapter 4) approach, referring to a dominant, or hegemonic masculinity, which nevertheless allows for the existence of varying forms of masculinity in different circumstances.

Such theoretical views have encouraged sociologists to begin asking questions about the varying types of masculinity and the conditions which promote them. Mac an Ghaill's collaborator **Christian Haywood**, has recently produced some interesting research relevant to this issue, examining the use of sexual slang as a form of abuse by rival groups of male pupils. Haywood's research in a mixed sixth form identified different groups of boys: one group he termed 'Dominant Heterosexuals', another group he termed 'Academic Achievers'. The 'Dominant Heterosexuals' frequently referred to 'Academic Achievers' as 'wankers', 'gays', 'poofs', whilst the 'Academic Achievers' attempted to resist this negative labelling and the version of masculinity which went with it, by terming the 'Dominant Heterosexuals' as 'cripples', 'cabbages' or 'spanners'. This research (which can be usefully compared to Sue Lee's work on reputational labelling), indicates that different versions of masculinity are developed by young men depending upon their position in an academic hierarchy, and indeed reminds us of the continued importance of class differences.

The examples discussed here indicate the changing ways in which gender influences culture and identity. Modernist sociology. in referring to 'individuals', has tended to delete gender differences. The recent interest in gender relations has led some sociologists to point out that all individuals are 'embodied', that is, to state the obvious, they have bodies! Obvious perhaps, but an area frequently neglected by sociologists who have, until recently, accepted the common sense view that the study of the body is something best left to biologists.

Study point
• What is the difference between gender and sex?

CULTURE, IDENTITY AND THE BODY

Recent theoretical and empirical work by sociologists has focused upon the significance of the human body in culture, and the way in which the body may be represented in a certain way, or used to create a sense of identity for individuals and groups. In a sense the body is yet one more resource which can be used to create a certain sort of identity, just as money can be used to buy expensive clothes to create another sort of identity. The topic of the body is closely related to discussion of gender, since one of the ways in which gender differences are expressed and created is through the body.

For some men this may be expressed in terms of the idea of 'hardness', whilst others may focus more on health and fitness, perhaps reflecting class-based differences in definitions of masculinity. At its most extreme the ideal form of male body is represented by the exaggerated figures of male body builders. One sociological interpretation of body building would be that it provides a means for some men to gain status and create a sense of identity around their particular notion of masculinity.

MASCULINITY AND THE BODY

There is a growing sociological literature describing how men's bodies are used in particular ways by men to reflect a sense of masculinity. Participation in sport is a key method for men to express masculinity. **Lenskyj**'s study, shows how physical achievement is predominantly seen in western societies as a male preserve. A whole set of cultural practices have grown up around many sports which work in a way that excludes women, thus emphasising the masculine nature of sport. Thus Lenskyj notes the culture of 'the locker room', with its sexually explicit songs and jokes, (especially those relating to homosexuality). Many sports have for a long time refused to allow women to participate. As Lenskyj comments, such practices have the effect of creating a clear distinction between men and women, and in reinforcing the view that differences between men and women are natural and inevitable. Lenskyj notes though, that women are not excluded from all sports; rather certain sports, such as ice-skating, synchronised swimming and netball, for instance, are represented as being particularly feminine, due to their need for graceful athleticism rather than muscular power. Lenskyj also observes, that where women do break with convention, they are frequently represented as particularly unfeminine, 'butch' or 'macho'.

Attitudes to black masculinity

Andrew Parker's recent study argues that notions of masculinity have frequently been racist. As Parker describes it, 'black bodies' have been negatively constructed. Historically this has worked in various ways, from an assumption of the innate superiority of the 'white races', to fears of the 'animal' sexuality of the 'black' male, to the more recent view that 'blacks' are somehow naturally more predisposed to have sporting talents.

R Majors' study demonstrates how many black males in the USA have indeed turned to sport as a key means of social mobility, and in so doing have created a particular style of masculinity, which Majors terms the 'cool pose', copied by other black males. Majors explains black involvement in sport, and the resulting style of masculinity which comes from it, as a result of status frustration (see Chapter 3). For young black men in the USA, unable to act out other versions of masculinity, by gaining occupational status for instance, sport has been one alternative route to success. For others less fortunate, the style of the 'cool pose' offers some way of responding to the dominant culture.

The 'new man'

A view of masculinity which has now been popular for some time is the idea of the 'new man'. Largely the creation of journalists, it has been argued that the 1980s saw the creation of a new, more sensitive and caring man, who felt constrained by the conventions of masculinity, and wished to be more emotional, and more expressive. Sociologists such as **Frank Mort** have indeed noted changes in the norms of masculine behaviour. Mort for instance has shown how in the 1980s a whole range of 'men's grooming products' – aftershave, hair gel, for instance – became available and acceptable to men. However, it is notable that such changes were brought about by closely tying such products to established cultural norms of male behaviour. They are frequently promoted by 'tough' male sports celebrities (see also Chapter 9).

Activity
Examine a range of popular newspapers and magazines. Produce evidence from them to show how men's grooming products are associated with toughness and those of women with femininity.

WOMEN, PORNOGRAPHY AND THE BODY

It would not be an exaggeration to argue that women's identity is centrally formed by the way the female body is regarded in our culture. Indeed many would argue that women, much more than men, are frequently judged by their appearance, rather than other more relevant characteristics. Feminists would argue that this is the result of a patriarchal culture, within which women are seen in terms of a 'male gaze'. Feminists such as **Andrea Dworkin** and **Catherine Mackinnon** would argue that nowhere is this aspect of our culture more prominently displayed than in the phenomenon of pornography. Their work provides substantial agreement as to the sociological significance of pornography. As Dworkin argues, pornography as an aspect of popular culture is produced wholly from a male viewpoint. It has the effect of 'objectifying' women and their sexuality, that is it turns them into mere objects which exist to provide pleasure for men – women are thus dehumanised by pornography. Catherine Mackinnon extends this argument, suggesting that women are defined as sexual objects by men in all areas of social life, not just pornography. Thus women's sexuality is defined by patriarchal culture in such a way as to limit the range of identities open to women. Women, Mackinnon claims, are seen by men primarily as sexual objects not just in the private sphere, but also in the workplace, the media and so on.

There is of course debate as to whether patriarchal culture exploits or empowers women: some women for instance, may argue that pornography provides a way for women to exercise power over men, to use their bodies against patriarchy. Recent debates about the pop singer Madonna reflect these different views. **Douglas Kellner** argues that Madonna simply provides cheap popular culture for the masses, whilst **Camille Paglia** sees Madonna as helping to rid women of guilt in expressing female sexuality. Feminist sociologists could argue that Madonna is not truly freeing herself from patriarchal culture, since her identity is still centred around her sexuality; she has simply succeeded in making herself better at a game whose rules have been created by men. She has not abolished the game.

CULTURE, IDENTITY AND EATING

A key point made by sociologists interested in the body, is the idea that people actively try to control and mould their body, in order to create their own sense of identity. One of the most obvious ways in which we do this is by eating food. Eating is of course a physical necessity, but it is an activity which is very much influenced by our culture.

- **Anthony Giddens** points out that drinking a cup of coffee is not simply an action which is done to quench thirst; it fulfils a social role, as for instance a gesture of welcome. Food thus takes on a differing significance depending upon gender.
- **Susie Orbach**'s book, *Fat is a Feminist Issue*, makes this point clear. It is mainly (though not exclusively) young women who become anorexic, and Orbach argues that it is patriarchal culture which creates the intense pressure to have a slim body, which then leads some women to become anorexic.
- Studies by **Keil, Murcott, Charles** and **Kerr**, argue that food has an influence

on men's and women's identities in other ways. It is for example generally seen as part of a woman's role to prepare food for a family. Eating food is a cultural activity, and the giving and eating of food can be seen as symbolising affection. In addition there are powerful norms and values at work to indicate appropriate foods for men and women. Charles and Kerr for instance point out how traditionally men get the best food. In working class families meat has been seen as essential for the 'breadwinner', given the physical nature of men's work. Correspondingly, a meal without meat may not be considered a 'proper meal', and vegetables and dishes without meat may be seen as suitable only for women. It is not therefore surprising that vegetarianism can be seen as a form of weakness, a lack of manliness, in some versions of masculinity. In this way, vegetarianism can be seen as a form of deviance from cultural norms and values.

Study point

- Suggest ways of illustrating the idea that eating food is influenced by social culture and is often symbolic.

THE BODY AND IMPAIRMENT

The sociologist **Tom Shakespeare** has argued that women's bodies are defined in relation to men's bodies: that is, they are judged negatively, in terms of how their bodies are not simply different, but also inferior to those of men. In the same way, those who are disabled, or impaired, are also negatively judged. The media invariably portray disability as a misfortune. The disabled are frequently shown as deserving of charity, or in some cases in literature or film, as evil. Shakespeare argues that our culture objectifies the disabled, just as women are objectified. There is a fetishism of the body (see Chapter 4), which leads to the disabled being treated as things, or objects, not as people.

Shakespeare explains these cultural values and the cultural representation of the disabled through several key points:

- It is masculine culture which seeks perfection in the human body, and indeed which is afraid of our mortality.
- It is because the disabled remind the so-called 'able bodied' of the frailty of life, and the inevitability of decay and eventual death, that the disabled have a stigmatised identity (see Chapter 5).
- Disability is socially constructed, and it is society which disables people.

- It is not the case that the disabled cannot do anything for themselves, rather, it is the rest of society which prevents and excludes the disabled from participation in many aspects of everyday life, even down to the mundane level of making it difficult for people to get into buildings.

It is for this reason that Shakespeare prefers to use the term 'impairment', rather than disability. As Shakespeare notes, all bodies are impaired in some way, and most of us will eventually experience further impairment as our bodies decay and eventually die.

This last point raises the issue of age and the lifespan. This may seem an area where at last sociological explanations are redundant, as birth and death must surely be seen as the most natural of life events. However, culture also shapes our understanding of, and attitudes towards, age.

Study point

- Suggest evidence supporting or refuting the view that the disabled have a stigmatised identity.

AGE, CULTURE AND MODERNITY

Age is an aspect of stratification which has frequently been neglected by sociologists. More recently however, sociologists have acknowledged that industrialised societies, as well as being stratified by class, gender and ethnicity, are also stratified by age. Age has a crucial bearing on our status and identity, since it determines whether and what sort of employment we can gain, whether we can marry, and indeed the sort of leisure activities we can participate in, determining whether we can go into pubs and clubs, the sorts of films we can watch, and even which sports and pastimes we can take part in.

Many sociologists would now agree that the way western societies mark age chronologically is culturally specific, and indeed a particular characteristic of industrialised societies. Thus we refer to 'eighteen year olds', and 'seventy year olds'. We also have implicit assumptions concerning at what age a person may be considered an adult, when they are middle-aged, and when they old. This is how our culture describes and measures age. Concepts of age are not fixed as cross cultural comparison indicates. In many cultures, such as the Hausa and the Chisunga of Africa, it has been puberty which marks the beginning of adulthood, not age in years.

Hockey and James argue that the western conceptualisation of age is something which largely came about with the development of industrial society. In pre-industrial society, where the family could be considered a unit of production, a person's age was not such a crucial determinant of their ability to work. Children for instance, were less likely to lead such a privileged existence as they were to come to have in industrial society, and were more likely to join in and help in productive activity. Hockey and James, drawing on a wide range of historical evidence, argue that industrialisation led to the exclusion of children, the elderly, and indeed women, from paid employment. Hockey and James argue that the exclusion of these categories of people from paid employment was the result of a desire for status which started amongst the aspiring middle classes and worked its way down into the working classes. This was a result of the desire of the middle classes to emulate the leisurely lifestyle of the aristocracy, and it became desirable, and indeed symbolic of one's social status, to demonstrate that one did not need to work. This view was also adopted by the working classes, and expressed through the trade unions as a demand for a 'family wage' for male workers. In due course, the nineteenth century trade unions did indeed achieve this aim. The effects of such aspirations however, were to make the elderly, the very young, and women, the dependents of men.

CULTURE, IDENTITY AND INFANTILISATION

Hockey and James argue that it is dependency which has led to a culture which 'infantilises' the young and the old. By this they mean that our culture turns the young and the old into infants who are by definition unable to act independently. The young and the old are seen as incapable of controlling their own bodies, and thus according to dominant cultural stereotypes, have to be cared for by adult carers. Hockey and James support their argument by research carried out by participant observation in an old people's residential home, as well as more theoretical work, and as they readily acknowledge, personal experience. Their work provides strong evidence that the elderly and the young have stigmatised identities; neither are considered to be completely 'proper' individuals due to their dependency on others. These stigmatised (or spoilt) identities are created and reinforced by a culture which infantilises them.

Jennifer Hockey's research in an old people's home for instance, indicated the strategies that care staff would use to 'infantilise' residents. Care staff, and indeed other residents, referred to the particularly frail elderly as the 'little people', or referred to their living area as the 'frail corridor'. If residents attempted to express any interest in sexuality, staff would use humour and gently or otherwise indicate that sexuality is an improper subject of interest for the elderly. In so doing, it can be argued that care assistants simply reflect the dominant ageism of our culture, which denies that elderly people are sexual beings. Hockey and James make similar points about the image of children in western cultures. The sexuality of children, like that of the elderly, is denied. Children are idealised and romanticised, being generally seen as innocent and incapable of looking after themselves. Such beliefs are reinforced by the images of both the elderly and children in the media. Hockey and James quote several examples from anthropological studies however, which indicate that these are views particular to western industrialised culture. The Sherbro of Sierra Leone for instance, treat the infirm elderly, and particularly those with incoherent speech, as especially sacred. The Sherbro believe that such elders are in touch with their ancestors. Moreover, as **Margaret Mead** and many other anthropologists have found, other cultures do not always share the view that child sexuality is taboo.

Study point

- Suggest some of the ways in which the young and the old have stigmatised identities.

Although the study of age has been relatively neglected by sociologists, one area which has received considerable attention has been youth subcultures. Functionalist sociologists, such as the American sociologist **Eisenstadt** in the late 1950s, were keen to study the 'new' phenomenon of youth culture. The prosperity which followed the Second World War, and the creation of a long period prior to starting work and adult life, has been seen as leading to the development of a range of youth cultures in the twentieth century. Eisenstadt provided a functionalist analysis of this development, and saw youth culture as society and young people's way of dealing with an extended period of time when adult status was denied to the young. Youth culture was thus seen in such functionalist analyses as a way of dealing with status frustration (see Chapter 3). One of the main criticisms of the functionalist analysis of youth culture, was that it neglected class differences between young people, which could make their experiences of youth very different. Other sociologists, such as those associated with the Birmingham University CCCS, produced an alternative analysis, which suggested that much of the cultural activity of young people reflected their resistance and opposition to capitalist culture (see Chapter 4). Contemporary sociologists would emphasise the variety of youth subcultures, and the way they reflect differences of class, gender and ethnicity.

Sociological analysis thus provides strong evidence for the claim that age is indeed socially constructed. This insight does not imply that the physiological changes associated with ageing are unimportant, but rather suggests that it is important to understand social attitudes and beliefs about age.

POINTS OF EVALUATION

This topic provides frequent opportunities for students to demonstrate their understanding of the relationship between sociological theory and research findings.

- The frequent stress in recent research on the variety of forms which masculinity and femininity can take has led some researchers to emphasise that sociologists should take care not to overgeneralise.

Mac an Ghaill refers to masculinities and femininities, acknowledging the way in which class, ethnicity, gender and age may interrelate. Some sociologists would now argue that the way in which these elements of stratification may be linked together makes it problematic to talk in general terms of masculinity or femininity, since what these terms mean and the identities which they lead to may vary, depending on class and ethnicity.

- It is also instructive to relate many of the studies discussed in this chapter to the role of the structure/action debate in the area of culture and identity. Many of the studies mentioned here show how people interpret and react to cultural norms and values.

Sylvia Walby makes the important observation that much sociological theory tends to see socialisation as a passive process, where individuals simply accept the identity and roles presented to them. Moreover in terms of gender, these roles are often understood to be mirror opposites. Male and female are thus understood as opposites of each other, with men for instance seen as being strong and unemotional, whilst women are portrayed as physically weak and emotional. Such views are inaccurate portrayals of reality and, as Walby argues, present a view of people as cultural dopes. Walby refers here to the tendency of structural theories to assume that people unquestioningly accept cultural roles and rules in shaping their identities.

- Lastly, it is always worth using sociological terminology to underline sociological understanding. The sociological view that gender is socially constructed rather than the result of natural differences has led to the term 'gendered identity'. Thus sociologists may refer to occupations being 'gendered', or talk of the 'gendering of work'.

SUMMARY

This chapter has shown how the feminist critique of malestream sociology has led to a greater insight into the ways in which culture is 'gendered'. It also shows how feminism has led sociologists to focus upon other issues, such as age and the body. The view that modernist sociology is not as objective and value-neutral as it sometimes claims has also been made by 'Black' sociologists, who argue that sociology has predominantly seen modern societies from the perspective of the dominant ethnic groups, that is 'white' people. This issue will be examined in the next chapter.

STUDY GUIDES

Group Work

1 Use a variety of popular magazines to examine images of men, women and the body. Do magazines tend to portray stereotypical images? What influence do you think magazine images have upon the construction of individual identity?

2 Debate the motion 'All women are exploited by pornography, whether they realise it or not'.

3 In groups, make a list of your daily activities, eg where you go, how you travel, what you eat. Imagine that you are wheelchair bound and unable to speak. How would you be able to carry on with your everyday life? Discuss and note down the effects which your impairment might have both practically, and in terms of how others perceive you.

Practice questions

ITEM A

Neil reportedly sometimes fought with strangers after rowing with someone he was close to: 'It's like if I had an argument with a close, like someone in the family, like I'd go out at night. And you start clicking it over, and someone can knock you. And you, you'll hit 'em. Cos like, them bigger than you. And it's like, you're getting back at yourself for the fight.' After hurting people he cared about, Neil wanted 'someone to come and hurt' him. Rather than verbally discussing differences with the person they rowed with, these young men displaced their anger on to a physical level and towards another less important person.

Joyce Canaan, in Mac an Ghaill, Understanding Masculinities, Open University Press, 1996, p121

ITEM B

From the age of six years old I attended a residential school for disabled children.[...] I was about 14 years old and had just finished preparing a salad in the cookery class. The teacher came over and said, ' What a good job you have made of that. You would have made someone a good wife.' 'What do you mean, I would have?' I asked. 'Well,' she replied, 'What I meant to say was if you marry a disabled man, you would make him a good wife.' The school had really strange ideas on marriage and the disabled. They believed that if a disabled person got married it should be to another disabled person as it would not be fair on an able-bodied person to burden them with a handicapped partner. Anyway an able-bodied person would not fancy a disabled person. I didn't go along with this idea at all. I knew for a fact that able-bodied boys fancied me. I had proved that when I went home for weekends.

Coyle, A, Husband, C, and Campling, J, in Anderson and Ricci, Society and Social Science – A Reader, Open University Press, 1990, p168

1 Assess to what extent sociological evidence supports the view that gendered identities in contemporary society are increasingly diverse. (8)
2 With reference to Item A and elsewhere, explain why men may find it difficult to express themselves emotionally. (5)
3 Assess the usefulness of the term 'new man'. (8)
4 Using material from Item B and elsewhere, explain why bodily impairment frequently leads to stigmatised identity. (4)

Coursework

1 Mac an Ghaill argues that increases in male unemployment and the increase in female semi-skilled employment has led to an identity crisis for many working class men. Is there evidence that this is the case in the area in which you live or study?
2 Undertake a study to observe and record the ways in which young men and women establish their senses of identity in the area in which you live or study. Have these changed over time? Make use of participant observation as well as interviews and other existing data. Note the changing youth cultures which have occurred and had some influence.
3 Undertake a study to examine the hypothesis that the disabled have a stigmatised identity.

8

CULTURE, IDENTITY AND ETHNICITY

Introduction

Table 7: *Theorists, concepts and issues in this chapter*		
KEY THEORISTS	KEY CONCEPTS	KEY ISSUES
• Tariq Modood	Ethnicity	Are some ethnic cultures more dominant than others within the nation-state?
• Waqar Ahmad	Race	
• Miri Song	Racism	Which are the more important influences upon the formation of ethnic identity – cultural or economic factors?
• Judy Scully	Nationalism	
• Stuart Hall	Nation-state	
• Rosemary Hill	Globalisation	Is globalisation leading to a greater mix of ethnic cultures (cultural hybridity) and a more multi-cultural society?
• Paul Gilroy	Cultural hybridity	
• David Cannadine	New cultural racism	
	Assimilation	
	Multi-culturalism	

THIS CHAPTER EXAMINES the way in which culture is related to ethnicity and race, and indeed the ways in which these terms are defined. The way in which culture and race become associated with the national cultures of nation-states is also considered, as are contemporary debates about nationalism and the changing nature of both racism and ethnic cultural identity. This last point involves asking whether British society is still racist, and if so in what way, and also the question of whether what some call 'ethnic minority' groups are gradually adopting the culture of the indigenous population.

MODERNITY AND ETHNICITY

In traditional societies, it can be argued that cultural identity was largely influenced by membership of small scale social groups such as tribes, or larger groups such as 'peoples', for example the Celts, who may have been settled over a range of discrete geographical sites, and could be governed by different administrative authorities. Differences between 'races' were not of course, unheard of in traditional society prior to industrialisation in the eighteenth century. However, prior to industrialisation and modern society, the differences between different 'races', at least from the white Northern European perspective, could have been explained in terms of natural differences, and these would have been seen as being ordained by God. Thus the European explorers and slave traders from at least the fourteenth century onwards, could justify their treatment of people from Africa and elsewhere by arguing that they were 'primitive' or 'savage'.

In many ways however, the coming of modern industrial society did not improve this situation, rather, it simply changed the justification for exploitation. Darwin's theory of evolution, developed in the nineteenth century, argued that all species, including humans, evolve over time through the process of natural selection, which led to the 'survival of the fittest'. In the nineteenth century, and indeed beyond, this was interpreted as implying the natural superiority, intellectually and physically, of white Europeans. Moreover, modern societies saw identity increasingly formed within the nation, rather than other groups such as tribes or peoples. When Western European nations (and the USA) grew in economic and military power, sometimes conquering poorer societies and countries and creating empires, belief in their own superiority, not surprisingly, grew as well. Membership or citizenship of these nations, and the associated benefits and rights, was not open to all; strict immigration laws and legislation regarding employment rights developed alongside the growth of the modern nation-state. Whilst modern nation-states were swift to proclaim their beliefs in democracy and equality, (for instance the French Declaration of the Rights of Man and Citizen, or the American Declaration of Independence), it is clear that they had a limited understanding of who counted as an individual.

ETHNOCENTRICISM, MODERNITY AND SOCIOLOGY

Just as feminists have argued that modernist sociological theories were 'gender blind', so more recently have other sociologists argued that they were 'race blind'. The 'founding fathers' of sociology, Marx, Durkheim, and Weber, largely took it as granted that the key aspect in forming the identity of the modern individual was class, and consequently had much less to say about race. Modern academic sociology was after all the invention of white European males, and largely focused upon the problems they were preoccupied with. Not surprisingly, they reflected the concerns, and to some extent the assumptions, of their time. Sociologists have recently drawn attention to the way this has meant that racial differences have been neglected, arguing that modern sociological theories have tended to assume that racial inequalities are the result of the class position of ethnic minority groups, and not simply of racial discrimination. It can be argued that modernist sociology has frequently been ethnocentric, a view which postmodernist theories have encouraged. Ethnocentricism refers to sociological theories, concepts, and research which predominantly concentrate upon one ethnic group; they thus become biased.

Critics of ethnocentricism would not only want to change the focus of much mainstream sociology, but would also want to emphasise the role which scholars from other ethnic groups made to the development of sociology. For example, scholars such as **William du Bois** (1868–1963), who was the first African-American to be awarded a Ph.D. from Harvard University in 1896, have been largely hidden from history, and have not received the acclaim given to other prominent sociologists. In the case of du Bois, it can be suggested that this is not the result of the lack of worth of his work, but rather reflects the biases of an ethnocentric sociology. Far from producing work of little importance, it was du Bois who, in contradiction to the analysis of Marx, argued that race would not become a secondary and minor aspect of stratification. As **Stephen Small** notes, du Bois suggested another key source of conflict:

> *The problem of the twentieth century is the problem of the colour line – the relation of the darker to the lighter races of men in Asia and Africa, in America and the islands of the sea.*

Sociology itself, whatever the intentions of its founders, has mainly promoted the views of a restricted and privileged group.

MODERNITY, SCIENCE AND ETHNICITY

The Palestinian academic and literary critic **Edward Said** has argued that notions of the superiority of the Europeans over other ethnic groups has long been a pervasive and persistent feature of Western thought. Said points out how Western thought has persistently denigrated those from other cultures as 'primitives', and 'savages', whilst neglecting the history of great civilisations, such as the Inca's, which predated the rise of Western culture. Moreover, in the view of Western cultures, those from the Orient (the East) were seen, stereotypically, as exotic and mysterious. Other characteristics were also imputed to these cultures, such as the belief that they were ruthless and put a much lower value on life than Westerners. The sociologist **Stuart Hall** has suggested that this has created a cultural climate where 'west' is always best. There has in other words, been a strong assumption in modern Western cultures that they were superior to 'other' cultures, particularly those from outside the 'west', that is Europe and the USA.

MEDICAL SOCIOLOGY

The implications of such a cultural assumption can have a profound influence upon the way a society functions, as can be illustrated by research into medical sociology by British sociologist **Waqar Ahmad**. Ahmad's research provides a good example of the way in which British (and Western) culture denigrates and misunderstands other cultures.

Ahmad's work examines the way recent research in medical sociology has conceptualised the use of traditional forms of medicine (these could be termed 'folk medicine') as 'a problem'. As a critical discipline, sociology has as its aim the goal of uncovering who has the power to make such definitions and rules, and the functions they play. As Ahmad explains, the word *hakim* broadly means scholar, and the fact that this name is used for healers in India and Pakistan reflects the holistic approach taken to medicine and health in traditional culture of these countries. *Hakims* practice a form of medicine which is usually called *hikmat*, although the terms *tibb*, *Unani* medicine, and *tibb-e-unani*, are also used. *Hikmat* is based on the theory of the four humours, derived from Hippocrates. This assumes that the human constitution is based upon the four humours of blood, phlegm, black bile and yellow bile, all of which have to be maintained in the correct balance. *Hikmat* is generally used by Muslims, whilst Hindus and Sikhs use a similar form of medicine and are treated by a *vaid*, rather than a *hakim*.

Ahmad makes several points about research conducted upon the role of the *hakim* and health in Asian communities. Firstly, Ahmad suggests that researchers tend to assume and probably overestimate the extent of the use of this form of medicine amongst Asian groups. Secondly, Ahmad points out that this has led researchers to assume that many Asian patients will visit both a *hakim* and a GP and will thus be likely to be receiving two sets of medication, with obvious dangers to their health. Thirdly, Ahmad points to a body of government-sponsored research, which identifies *hakim* remedies as being responsible for high levels of lead in the blood of Asian children.

Ahmad is critical of all of the assumptions and implications of such research. Ahmad can be seen to be arguing that the use of *hikmat* may actually not be that prevalent amongst Asians, and to suggest that it is reflects a stereotype which portrays Asians as 'primitive'. To suggest that Asian patients will be using two sets of medication, Ahmad argues, is to imply that any consequent illness amongst Asian patients is their own fault. As Ahmad argues, there is no evidence to suggest that Asians are any more likely to be using other treatments than other groups in the population, especially given the popularity of alternative medicine. On this point then, the issue is why Asians should be singled out for criticism. On the matter of levels of lead in the blood, Ahmad points out that there is not a consensus amongst medical researchers as to whether *hikmat* medicines such as *surma* (an eye cosmetic used for eye conditions), really are the cause of such high levels of lead in the blood. Ahmad cites evidence from a study which indicates that high levels of lead in the blood are in fact the result of living in inner city areas, where much of the Asian population is concentrated.

Study point
● Examine official statistics on health with respect to ethnic minority groups. Include infant mortality rate, standard mortality rate and long term illnesses. What social and cultural factors might influence the health of ethnic minorities?

Finally, Ahmad is critical of the notion implicit in previous research into *hikmat* medicine which, he argues, implies that it is problematic and scientifically invalid. Ahmad sees this as cultural arrogance (once again Asians are perceived as a problem) , and another illustration of the view that 'west is best'. Alternative medicine is growing in popularity, so Ahmad's work can be seen to raise the question as to why Asian medicine is perceived as a particular problem. *Hikmat* is portrayed as unscientific and yet, Ahmad argues, the many failures, dangers and errors of Western medicine are conveniently neglected by those who criticise *hikmat*. Ahmad does not suggest that *hikmat* is superior or infallible, but simply wishes to argue for tolerance, and for criticism to be based upon systematic research into the efficacy of *hikmat*. Ahmad's study indicates that those who assume that science is neutral in its treatment of culture and race are mistaken. Science may present itself as being neutral and objective, but values, which are cultural, cannot be eradicated. A similar point can be made of sociology, however, and this is evident in the terminology used by sociologists to discuss issues of race and ethnicity.

Study point

Use CD-Rom and other sources to investigate the popularity of alternative medicine. To what extent are such therapies used exclusively by members of minority ethnic groups?

MODERNITY, SOCIOLOGY AND ETHNICITY

Many would argue that in spite of its shortcomings, modernist sociology has provided a good foundation for the study of race and ethnicity. Indeed, it could be pointed out that in contrast to sociobiological theories, which have offered a view of racial differences as being the result of natural differences between very different types of human being, modernist sociological theories have at least put the case that race is a socially constructed category, which has no real scientific validity. Such a view has been proposed by sociologists such as **Michael Banton**, and by geneticists such as **Steve Jones** and **Steven Rose**, both of whom have argued that the biological or genetic differences between different so-called 'races' are not scientifically significant.

THE SOCIOLOGICAL STUDY OF RACE

Before examining how modernist's treatment of race and ethnicity have been criticised, it is important briefly to outline some of the achievements of the sociological study of race. Sociologists studying race have contributed significantly to our understanding of race and ethnicity, and have also contributed to combatting racism. Much research in Britain from the 1960s onwards, focused upon examining the causes of the discrimination suffered by ethnic minorities in employment, education and housing. This research (eg **Rex** and **Moore**, Rex and **Tomlinson**, **Smith** and **Gray**) certainly succeeded in demonstrating the reality of discrimination in all these areas. Modernist sociologists might well feel justified in asking 'what's the problem?'

The sociologist **Tariq Modood** has presented a detailed critique of the way sociology has tackled the study of race, which suggests that there have indeed been a variety of problems with the way race has been studied. Modood has noted that sociologists have predominantly used terms such as 'black' to describe all ethnic groups. Thus Asian groups have had an identity imposed upon them, from the outside, so to speak. Furthermore, Modood argues, there has been a tendency to think that 'race' essentially means the same as skin colour. Thus, when white sociologists talk about 'Asians' as a racial group, they imply that because they are of the same skin colour, they are members of one social group.

Modood points out that for 'Asians', 'race' is more likely to be defined in terms of culture or religion. By making this distinction, Modood is able to recognise the diversity of ethnic groups amongst 'Asians', which is used as a blanket term. The category 'Asians' would include different nationalities such as Bangladeshis, Pakistanis, Indians and Asians from Africa, as well as different religious groups, Sikhs, Muslims, Hindus, and several main language groups, including Gujarati, Punjabi, Urdu and Kutchi.

In general terms, Modood argues that it is important to recognise the complexity of ways in which class, culture and colour intersect. This recognition emphasises the differences within and between ethnic groups, and is thus an aid to understanding social phenomena with greater accuracy. Modood's analysis would suggest that modernist sociology has had a tendency to ethnocentricism. One implication of this might be that it would be preferable to allow ethnic groups to define themselves, rather than to impose categories upon them. As a consequence of arguments such as Modood's, contemporary sociologists are starting to look with greater sensitivity at differences within so-called ethnic minority groups, and the term 'new ethnicities' is becoming used more frequently to refer to the wider range of groups studied. These points can be extended further. It is increasingly being recognised that the sociological study of ethnicity needs to be extended from the narrow preoccupation with 'black' groups, to study other groups. Thus sociologists have recently studied Chinese communities and other ethnic groups. Recent changes in Britain have even raised interesting questions about English ethnic identity (see p 110).

Activity
Examine official statistics and if possible census data on ethnic minorities in Britain. What criticisms could be made of ethnic categories used by government research?

Explanations of ethnic inequality

The usefulness of the criticisms suggested from the above activity can be illustrated by brief reference to the treatment of race and ethnicity by some of the major sociological perspectives. It can be suggested that all of the major structural perspectives have crucial weaknesses in explaining ethnic inequalities in the areas of employment, educational attainment and housing. Marxism, with its focus upon class, has tended to see race as less important than class. Marxist explanations of ethnic disadvantage have therefore tended to argue that ethnic minorities' disadvantages are a result of their membership of the working class, and not primarily as a result of their race. Similarly, Weberian explanations have argued that ethnic disadvantage is the result of ethnic minority workers being concentrated in a secondary labour market, and this can then be applied to explain other inequalities in lifechances faced by members of ethnic minority groups. Lastly, liberal theories (which are broadly comparable in this context to functionalist explanations), have argued that ethnic disadvantage (particularly in employment) is the result of lower levels of skill and training which immigrants inevitably tend to have. Liberal theory is, however, optimistic that over time inequalities are reduced, as ethnic minorities 'work their way up'.

It can be suggested that all these theoretical explanations fail to provide an adequate explanation of ethnic inequality, primarily because they fail to consider race or ethnicity as a sufficiently important explanatory concept, preferring in general to prioritise class differences. In this sense all of the above theories could be described as 'race (or colour) blind'. This is not to imply that the above theories have no use whatever in the analysis of ethnic disadvantage; **Robert Miles** has attempted to apply Marxist concepts in this task, whilst the work of **John Rex** has attempted to do the same with Weberian theory. However, critics such as Modood would no doubt suggest that the failings of these theories is an almost inevitable outcome of prioritising economic categories over cultural categories. It can be suggested that more adequate sociological analysis has to involve both cultural and economic categories (Modood's notion of class, colour, and culture).

It can therefore be suggested, that to use exclusively economic categories runs the risk of denying the reality of racism. Put very crudely, it can be argued that the real cause of ethnic disadvanatage is simple: it is racism. Racism can be simply defined as any form of discrimination made on the basis of implied racial difference, and may occur at different levels within society. Thus, an individual may be racist, perhaps by acting in an aggressive manner or simply by making stereotypical assumptions about a person's behaviour. However, sociologists also use the term institutional racism, to refer to systematic biases and discriminations in the way institutions operate, however well intentioned those working in such institutions may be.

Study point
• Describe how a non-white person, for whom English is a second language, might experience British society as racist. Include institutional experiences in education, health, employment, religion and leisure.

THE TERMINOLOGY OF ETHNICITY

It is appropriate at this point, given the focus upon Modood's critique of the use of the term 'black', to comment a little further on the terminology used to discuss ethnicity in sociology, and indeed in society generally. There is much debate about the preferred terms to use to discuss ethnicity. Many sociologists prefer not to use the term 'race', since they argue that it carries the misleading view that there are such things as 'races'. As previously noted, geneticists such as Jones and Rose dispute the scientific basis of the term, and argue that it is not therefore a meaningful scientific category. Other sociologists have defended the use of term, since they argue that if it is used by people to describe their own identity, then it is useful for sociological analysis. Despite the criticisms of the term 'race', many continue to speak of racism, or racial discrimination, since this can imply that discrimination is made upon the basis of invalid characteristics imputed to a particular social group.

Yet others have preferred the use of the term 'ethnicity', since ethnicity refers to membership of a group with a shared culture. This term has the advantage of being applicable to all people, since it is not tied to skin colour. Both 'race' and 'ethnicity' are distinct from 'nationality', since it is possible for people to have the same passport but belong to different ethnic groups, eg Scots, Irish, Welsh, Punjabis, Gujaratis, Sikhs and English people holding a British passport. Some dislike the term 'ethnic minority', since it can imply marginal status and thereby easily sound condescending. There are no simple answers as to which terms are preferable, but it is an important issue of interpretation for students to note that sociologists' choice of terms cannot be value-neutral, and may reflect the cultural background and assumptions of the researcher.

Interestingly, the recent tendency to examine ethnicity in terms of culture is also reflected in the ways in which members of particular ethnic groups are increasingly discriminated against, purely because of the membership of a particular cultural group.

CULTURE, IDENTITY AND THE NEW CULTURAL RACISM

The sociologist **Paul Gilroy** has recently argued that there has been a change in the nature of racism, and indeed that there has been a shift from a biological to a cultural definition of race. Gilroy's views in part reflect the development of political debates on ethnicity in Britain. Arguably, politicians or other public figures would now find it very hard to express views which explicitly expressed the superiority of 'white' ethnic groups, without censure. In the early 1990s the Conservative politician Norman Tebbit reflected a new way of being racist when he argued that immigrants were welcome to Britain, as long as they ensured that their chief allegiance and loyalty was to Britain. The way Lord Tebbit expressed this was in terms of a sporting analogy, suggesting that Asians or West Indians who continued to support India, Pakistan or the West Indies cricket teams, rather than the English team, were lacking in loyalty to the nation which offered them citizenship. As such, Lord Tebbit appeared to imply, they could not expect full support, or perhaps citizenship, in return. Tebbit's comments provide a perfect illustration of Bauman's view of culture, which is that it is intrinsically aggressive, aiming to achieve dominance or hegemony over other cultures (see Chapter 2).

This can be seen as a much more sophisticated form of racism, given its apparent refutation of 'older' (though by no means, dead) forms of racism based upon 'scientific' beliefs in the superiority of certain racial groups. Gilroy argues however, that even those opposed to racism, so-called 'multi-culturalists', can believe in the idea of 'pure' or distinct and separate ethnic cultures. Gilroy argues that this is a fiction, and that sociologically, ethnicity can only be fully understood in the context of the development of the nation-state and nationalism.

Study point

- Consider how important ethnicity or nationality is to your own sense of identity. It may be unimportant, or perhaps only important at certain times. It's importance may vary in different contexts. Do you become very upset when your country's team loses? If so, what functions do you think your ethnic or national identity plays?

CULTURE, IDENTITY AND NATIONALISM

Nationalism is something which is frequently taken for granted, and the loyalties and identities which it leads to may not always be subjected to scrutiny, or may even be considered to be 'natural'. However, as the political scientist **David Marquand** has argued, the nation-state is a relatively recent creation, and nationalism has only become an important source of culture and identity with the development of the modern nation-state. A nation can be defined as a geographical area which is governed by one sovereign political authority, and whose members share a belief in some common identity. As **David Jary** notes, the territorial claims of a nation-state, tend to coincide with cultural and linguistic practices, and with ethnic divisions.

Stuart Hall describes how national cultures operate by using a variety of symbols of national unity, by inventing traditions, and by creating a range of myths and folklore, which portray national heroes. In short a whole mythology is created around the idea of a nation, which can then be used to encourage people to identify with the nation. The historian **David Cannadine** shows how, for instance, most of the rituals and ceremonial procedure surrounding the British monarchy in the twentieth century was mostly invented around the late nineteenth century. Around this time too, was developed the notion of the royal family as providing a role model for the nation, and a national moral figurehead.

REMEMBRANCE SUNDAY AT THE CENOTAPH IN LONDON

These critical insights into the nature of nationalism indicate that it is something which is socially constructed. The British nation was moulded from Irish, Welsh, Scottish and English ethnic groups, not to mention previous ethnic groups who migrated to the British Isles prior to the eighteenth century. In the twentieth century, migration has continued. British national identity then, and with it British culture, is not something which exists in some 'pure' state; it has always been a mix of different groups. As **Husband** points out, it is because of this that it can be argued that there is no one ideology of the nation which is shared by all citizens. This means, of course, that whilst in some general ways it may make sense to talk about a 'British identity' and a 'British culture', to do so begs important questions. Sociologists have been concerned to demonstrate how some ethnic groups have more power than others in defining what is to count as 'Britishness' in terms of culture and identity. The idea of cultural racism has already been explained, but an important illustration of the way ethnicity works in Britain has been provided by the debates around the novel *The Satanic Verses* by Salman Rushdie.

CULTURE, ETHNICITY, AND *THE SATANIC VERSES*

In 1988, the Indian born writer Salman Rushdie (educated at Rugby, the upper class public school, and Oxford University), published a novel titled *The Satanic Verses*, which satirised Muhammad, the sacred prophet and founder of the Islamic faith. The book was publicly burnt and the Muslim authorities called for Rushdie's death. In response to those who saw this as a 'fundamentalist' reaction, Modood observed that the majority of British Muslims who are Sunnis, are only fundamentalist in that they believe in the literal truth of the Quran. However, the particular sects of Sunnis amongst the British Muslim community are members of the Barelvis and Deobandis sects. Modood argues that the history of these groups in Pakistan and India demonstrates, if anything, rather apolitical traditions. Modood suggests that the passion and intensity of the protest against Rushdie owes more to the deep sense of cultural hurt felt by these groups as a result of the publication of *The Satanic Verses*. This hurt was experienced simply because religious faith is one of the key aspects of these groups' cultural identity. Modood points to the central importance of the family in what he calls 'South Asian' culture. This culture is one which has a very conservative view of the family. Sex is seen in a more traditional light, as something which is for procreation and the continuance of the family line, not for individual enjoyment. Modood also notes the importance of the family, and the biradari or kinship group, to a sense of identity, suggesting that this too, contributes to understanding the reaction to Rushdie's book. The sociologist **Anthony Giddens**, has, in contrast, defined fundamentalism as a 'refusal of dialogue'. and thus an insistence upon the truth of one's own particular beliefs (see Chignell and Abbott, 1995).

However, Modood also acknowledges the importance of class in the case of British Muslims. Modood claims that most South Asians (mainly Pakistanis and Bangladeshis) are only one generation away from living as a rural peasantry. They are now predominantly concentrated in low paid manual work in the North and Midlands; they consequently suffered considerably during the unemployment of the 1980s, and have missed out on the growth in the service sector in the 1980s and 90s. In contrast to some commentators, Modood argues that if an attempt is to be made to identify an ethnic underclass, this must qualify as such a group.

Some of the most important questions about ethnicity for sociologists, focus around whether minority ethnic groups will be assimilated, that is merged, into the wider society; whether they will be separated in some way, and thus maintain their own culture and identity, or whether they will be 'accommodated', with co-existence and tolerance leading to a multi-cultural society. Modood's analysis casts doubt upon the possibilities of a harmonious multi-culturalism or gradual assimilation. Recent research into ethnicity suggests that the situation is one of increasing complexity.

ETHNICITY AND GLOBALISATION

Recent research by sociologists has been influenced by ideas about the process of globalisation. Globalisation refers to the process whereby the world is increasingly interconnected in economic, social, political and cultural ways (see Chapter 9). In terms of ethnicity, globalisation has meant increased migration as, driven by various political and economic factors, people seek employment and a better standard of living. This process however, can also have effects upon culture and the nation-state. As Hall notes, these effects may work in a contradictory way. Globalisation may have several effects on ethnicity and identity. Firstly, it may lead to the eroding of a national culture, and the creation of a homogenous global culture, national cultures thus becoming more similar. Secondly, it may mean that national, or local (eg English, Irish), identities are strengthened, as local cultures attempt to resist globalisation. Thirdly, national cultures may decline, leading to new cultures and cultural identities. These last cultures are called cultures of hybridity, the word hybrid referring to the offspring of two different varieties of something, eg plants, animals, or cultures.

Stuart Hall argues that whilst the evidence for the first of these changes is rather unconvincing, there is evidence of the other two changes occurring. This of course, means that the resulting social conditions may provide some evidence of ethnic groups mixing harmoniously and some evidence of tensions, as the different cultures will be competing. Culture will therefore be contested, and so too will identity.

CULTURAL IDENTITY IN BRITAIN

This complex conclusion can be supported with evidence gathered by other sociologists. Many commentators in Britain during the post-Second World War period of immigration hoped for an assimilation of migrants into British culture. This of course implied that 'they'(immigrants) must become more like 'us' (the indigenous population). Many taking this view assumed that the children of immigrants would experience some 'culture clash' as the contradictions between the two different cultures they experienced were exposed. Another suggestion was that there would be generational conflict between migrants and their children, as children would increasingly want to adopt Western values, in the face of assumed parental opposition.

Drury's research into Sikh families indicates on the contrary that children in Sikh families find a variety of adaptations to the relationship between Sikh culture and the culture of the wider society, and noted very little conflict between the attitudes of parents and children. **Gardner** and **Shukur**, found that amongst young Bengalis allegiance to Islam was becoming more common, and argue that this is because it provides young Bengalis with a sense of support and provides a positive identity denied by white culture. **Rosemary Hill**'s research into the housing aspirations of the Asian communities in Leicester also notes the importance of cultural factors, and the continuity of cultural tradition amongst the young. Whilst previous sociological research, such as that of **Rex** and **Moore**, attempted to explain the residential segregation of ethnic minorities in terms of economic factors, Hill argues that both economic and cultural factors play a part. Hill used questionnaires and semi-structured interviews to examine how Asian families had made decisions about where to live, as well as their aspirations for the future. The study found that both old and young Asians liked living in an 'Asian community' as this allowed them to be close to friends and relatives, as well as temples, schools and shops run by those from a similar ethnic background. This was not however simply a matter of wealth, but rather a cultural issue. Many respondents commented upon how they felt freer to continue to practise their own cultural activities in an Asian neighbourhood, as opposed to one where they would be in a minority. Importantly, these were views broadly shared by young and old, and for many of the young, family commitments were given as an additional reason for remaining in an area. It was also notable that the two largest elements of the 'Asian' community, Muslims and Hindus, lived in different areas of the city, and tended not to mix.

As a result of the recent focus upon culture and the interest in cultural differences, sociologists have also started to examine a wider variety of ethnic groups. Research by **Miri Song** into the Chinese in Britain, and by **Judy Scully** into the Irish in America and Britain, are good examples of this new research. Miri Song argues that her research into Chinese families demonstrates that many second generation Chinese do see themselves in broad terms as influenced by both British and Chinese cultures, but that this is the result of both economic and cultural factors. An important determinant of cultural identity, Song claims, is the ways in which children contribute to the family unit through economic activity.

Song researched into the relationships between work, family and cultural identity amongst a sample of Chinese families running take-away businesses in South-east England. Structural economic factors have an important influence in determining the types of work available for the Chinese in Britain, and small businesses such as take-aways are one type of opportunity which exist. However, cultural factors also influence the identity of young people in that those children who do offer to 'help out' in the family business are not only labelled as 'good' children, but are also seen as being more Chinese (Chinese culture stresses the importance of family solidarity and collective duty and loyalty). Of course, Song observes, not all children are prepared to help out, and their cultural identity subsequently is less influenced by Chinese culture.

Judy Scully's research into the Irish, was conducted through interviews with 42 proprietors of bars in Birmingham UK and Chicago USA. Scully's research confirmed the interplay between structural and cultural factors in the construction of identity. Scully observes that there are strong cultural (and racist) stereotypes existing in both countries, which portray the pub as the natural home of the Irish, and the Irish people in general as being habitually drunk. Scully argues that these stereotypes of Irish identity can be used as a resource by bar owners, and in this sense, they become a form of cultural capital. Scully's research shows how Irish bar owners, along with their staff, adopt a 'stage Irish identity'. In other words, they live up to the stereotype of the Irish. This is done in various ways, but Scully notes particularly the cultivation of self-consciously 'Irish' accents, and allowing and actively promoting the bar's use as a meeting point ('home') for Irish people new to the country.

Whilst in some ways access to this cultural resource may seem to empower the Irish bar owner, since it provides them with their livelihood, Scully argues that at the same time it reinforces their marginal structural position in society. Scully also notes that most Irish bar owners find themselves in that type of work due to 'blocked mobility'; that is, the absence of other career paths as a result of their immigrant and ethnic cultural status.

Study point
• Suggest what sort of evidence could be used to indicate that Britain is becoming an increasingly multicultural society.

POINTS OF EVALUATION

The research outlined here provides some support for the view that in contemporary society there is both a strengthening of some national cultures, such as Asian, Muslim, Irish or Chinese and, at the same time, a decline in national identity and the development of hybrid cultures. Hall argues that this is the result of globalisation. The strengthening of particular national cultures and the changing of others, should not however, be surprising. Culture is after all a contested concept. All the particular cultures discussed here can be considered to be in competition with each other. Culture is something which is a process, rather than a static structure, and so cultures are always changing.

Various conclusions may be reached as to the implications of these changes for ethnicity and culture in Britain. Multi-culturalists might offer a relatively optimistic view of a new tolerance as the logical consequence of increasing cultural hybridity. However, sociologists such as Modood and **Small**, would argue for greater caution. As the 'new cultural racism' indicates, racism does not just have to be about colour. These changes are also occurring at a time when important questions about the nature of British culture and identity are also being raised by the various issues surrounding the European Union and devolution. Thus at the same time that attempts are made to strengthen 'British nationalism', other tensions are also making themselves felt in British society.

SUMMARY

The last three chapters have involved examining contemporary society and culture in terms of the key sociological concepts of class, gender and race. In the course of each chapter it has been indicated that considerable cultural changes have occurred within British society. Many sociologists have identified these changes as being common to societies throughout the world. It is now appropriate to try and describe the nature of these changes, and to evaluate the sociological interpretations made of them. The last chapter therefore, examines the sociological explanations, descriptions and debates about, contemporary society.

STUDY GUIDES

Group Work

1 Use a CD-Rom to access Norman Tebbit's comments on ethnicity and culture in *The Daily Telegraph* 6th October 1997 (use byline/author search – Robert Shrimsley). Do you agree with Norman Tebbit that the existence of different cultures in one society will inevitably lead to conflict?

2 Use CD-Rom to access an article by Vivek Chaudhary on Asian gangs in *The Guardian* 3rd May 1997. Does the article provide evidence for or against cultural hybridity? How might sociologists explain the conflict between the two gangs?

3 Debate the motion that 'Cultural hybridity is increasing in Britain'. Ensure that arguments both for and against the statement are supported with sociological evidence.

Practice questions

ITEM A

'Helping Out' in Chinese Take-away Businesses by Miri Song

> It seemed that both interviewees and I were concerned about being judged by the other: how Korean or Chinese, as opposed to American or British, were we perceived to be? Feelings of defensiveness or nervousness were engendered by fears that we were seen as not Korean or Chinese 'enough'. Two markers of cultural identity that seemed to require disclosure and justification were our language abilities and our intimate relationships with partners and friends.

> As with not being able to speak one's 'mother' tongue, having relationships with individuals who were not Chinese or Korean, was assumed to indicate a taboo 'defection'.

Adapted from Miri Song and David Parker, Commonality, Difference and the Dynamics of Disclosure in In-Depth Interviewing, Sociology, Vol 29, No 2, pp241–256, May 1995

ITEM B

...We could see quite clearly, as the teams warmed up before the kick-off, that banana after banana was being hurled from the away supporters' enclosure. The bananas were designed to announce, for the benefit of those unversed in codified terrace abuse, that there was a monkey on the pitch; and as the Liverpool fans have never bothered to bring bananas to previous Arsenal matches, even though we have always had at least one black player in the side since the turn of the decade, one can only presume that John Barnes was the monkey to whom they were referring.

Nick Hornby, Fever Pitch, Indigo 1996, p189

1   With reference to Item A, explain why language is such an important aspect of culture and cultural identity. (4)

2   Using information from Item A and elsewhere, explain how the ethnicity of the researcher may influence research findings. (5)

3   The material in Item A notes the taboo on relationships with those from a different culture. Briefly suggest why this is considered offensive within a culture. (2)

4   What were Liverpool supporters symbolising by throwing bananas and making monkey noises at John Barnes ? Refer to Item B. (2)

5   Suggest two criticisms which could be made of the use of the term 'black' to describe John Barnes. Suggest two reasons why such a description could be considered acceptable. (4)

6   Using information from the Items and elsewhere, evaluate the view that British culture is becoming culturally hybrid. (8)

Coursework

1   Conduct an investigation to determine whether cultural hybridity is occurring amongst an ethnic group. Compare norms and values between different generations.

2   Investigate the role of the family in maintaining cultural identity amongst an ethnic group.

3   Examine the portrayal and the symbols of British cultural identity used by newspapers and television. What are the functions of nationalism in British society?

9

CULTURE, IDENTITY AND CONTEMPORARY SOCIETY

Introduction

Table 8: *Theorists, concepts and issues in this chapter*		
KEY THEORISTS	KEY CONCEPTS	KEY ISSUES
• Jean Baudrillard	Postmodernism	What is postmodernism?
• Jean-Francois Lyotard	Grand theories	Are postmodernists right to emphasise the role of culture and consumption in contemporary society?
• Robert Bocock	Globalisation	
• Frank Mort	Hyperreality	Is postmodernism a useful theory?
• Sean Nixon	Simulacra	
• George Ritzer	Media saturation	
• Ulrich Beck	Consumer culture	
• David Harvey	Seduction	
• Frederic Jameson	Risk society	
• Anthony Giddens		

THIS CHAPTER EXAMINES the idea that contemporary society is undergoing fundamental social change. The sociological perspective most closely associated with this view is postmodernism. Not only does postmodernism argue that society is undergoing large scale social and cultural change, it also makes a number of criticisms of modernist sociological perspectives, which draw upon the criticisms raised in previous chapters. Whilst there are many valid criticisms which can be made of postmodernist theory, this chapter will suggest that the questions which postmodernists have raised are helpful ones, and that they do reflect real social and cultural change in contemporary society.

MODERNITY AND POSTMODERNITY

Sociology is a subject which was largely developed in the nineteenth century. This was also, of course, the period which witnessed the process of industrialisation. In Britain, the basically rural society of 1750 had turned into something very different in the space of a century. The grandparents of young adults in the 1890s would not have recognised their grandchildren's social world. Sociology developed over the same time, largely with the aim of trying to subject these social changes to scientific analysis. The idea was that since it had been scientific knowledge which had transformed industry and technology, a new science of society could find the solution to social problems such as crime and poverty.

More recently sociologists and social theorists have argued that modern societies are again undergoing substantial social change. Previous chapters have noted how sociologists have suggested that gender, ethnicity and class divisions are no longer as clearcut as modernist sociologists may have implied. In the case of all these aspects of stratification, some sociologists now argue that greater sensitivity to the full range of social differences is needed. Sociologists have directed their attention to other sources of identity, such as age and the body, and as will be demonstrated later in this chapter, consumption (consumerism, shopping) is now considered by many sociologists to be an important source of identity.

Postmodernists argue that capitalist societies have now changed so much, that to focus upon the economy and upon production is to fundamentally misunderstand them. Rather, postmodernists argue, sociologists should focus their attention upon consumption and culture. This, postmodernists argue, is because capitalism has been so successful that conflicts over the distribution of wealth pale into insignificance in the context of the affluent consumer society visible in many capitalist societies. Important social differences are now the result of different consumption choices, and a more complex interaction of class, ethnicity and gender. Sociologists need to study cultural meanings and symbolism, and identities, in this new context.

CHANGES IN CONTEMPORARY SOCIETY

Increasingly sociologists now tend to see modern society (modernity) in terms of a particular configuration of economic, political and social institutions.

Modern society

- Economically modern societies were concerned with mass production of standardised goods, epitomised in the twentieth century by Henry Ford's production line of cars, hence the term Fordism.
- In social terms modern societies were class societies, something which Marxists and functionalists could agree upon, although they disagree about whether class was functionally necessary, and its role in a capitalist division of labour.
- Politically these economic and social arrangements were both developed and defended by nation-states competing in a largely free market.
- Culturally, modern society was seen as divided very much on class lines, with clear distinctions between high culture and mass culture. Culture was not considered particularly important sociologically in this sort of society.
- In theoretical terms sociology was generally seen as attempting to study society in a scientific way, although this was always an issue of considerable debate.

Postmodern society

Postmodern societies on the other hand are characterised by a different institutional pattern.

- Economically, there has been a switch to 'small batch production' for niche markets. This is illustrated by the Japanese term *kanban* – just-in-time production (JIT), whereby companies produce a wide range of models, continually changing styles, colours, etc.
- Societies are no longer organised around the issue of production – what is important now, in a much wealthier society, is consumption. Thus classes and class identity (or class consciousness) is much less important than how people distinguish themselves and gain status through consumption.
- Politically, in the postmodern era the nation-state is being eclipsed by the rise of a global culture. In such a climate nation-states may lose their legitimacy. However, in the face of global culture – culture which is becoming the same the world over – there are frequent assertions of local identity. Thus in Eastern Europe following the collapse of communism (itself partly the result of the communist states' inability to withstand the economic pressures of global capitalism), the former Soviet Union has split into many smaller states on the basis of ethnic culture.
- There is a fragmentation of cultural boundaries. The differences between high and popular culture are blurred, partly since class itself is no longer the key organising feature of society.

POSTMODERNITY AND THE MASS MEDIA

The importance of a media created consumer culture is an idea which is reflected in the work of the postmodernist **Jean Baudrillard**. Baudrillard argues that contemporary society is 'media saturated'. So inundated are we by media symbols and messages, Baudrillard argues, that we have lost the ability to distinguish reality from fiction. We therefore live in a state of what Baudrillard terms hyperreality. Baudrillard's comments on the Gulf War of 1991 provide a controversial example of this. For Baudrillard the war, images of which were passed onto the public by the media, became similar to a computer game. The technology used was so powerful that television viewers could watch bombs and missiles homing onto their targets, while seated in their own living rooms. Viewers' though, were removed from the reality of the violence, and never saw any dead soldiers. Baudrillard thus argues that the media present us with 'simulacra', artificial images of what he argues are 'unreal' events, because they are so distorted and distanced from the reality. The 'reality' of a missile hitting its target is not shown to the television viewer; what they see is a simulacra of the real event. Baudrillard argues that this is what television generally does; it creates a distorted view of reality. Baudrillard calls this view of reality, hyperreality. The term hyperreality reflects the fact that media images try to be more 'real than reality', using a variety of techniques to make viewers feel that they are experiencing an event.

Activity

Conduct a short piece of research to examine whether there is evidence of 'media saturation'. How well informed are a sample of people about: major news issues; pop charts; football results and league positions; latest developments in a range of soap opera's; current adverts and scandals in contrast to their knowledge about significant world events and matters of 'high culture'?

Is the implication that detailed knowledge of a more trivial kind is evidence of a dangerous commercial culture justified?

POSTMODERNITY AND GLOBALISATION

Globalisation refers to the notion that events in one society can now have very important influences upon other societies. The idea of the global economy provides a good example here. The world economy is now dominated by large 'trans-national corporations', whose operations are based in many different countries, rather than being confined to one nation. This means that the prospects of employment, and indeed the lifestyle and culture, of people in Sunderland is influenced in a direct way by decisions taken by the Nissan corporation in Japan (there is a large Nissan factory near Sunderland).

Globalisation can also refer to the general way in which people nowadays are able to consume a wide range of products from all over the world. We are able to buy food and clothes from all over the globe. The presence of mass media is also a global phenomenon, and British television viewers and cinema audiences are likely to watch many films and programmes made elsewhere in the world. Postmodernists argue that this creates a global culture. In other words, people all around the world will share a similar way of life, and probably watch the same films (made in Hollywood and customised for different markets), and television programmes.

Postmodernism has had a tremendous, although highly debated, influence on sociology. By its emphasis on economic, social and political change it has led sociologists to focus on issues of culture and identity, since it has been argued that we live in a society which is increasingly organised around consumption, and where individuals are able freely to choose their identity and lifestyle, unhampered by the old constraints of class, ethnicity or gender. By suggesting that we are witnessing the development, and indeed the triumph, of a global culture, the concept of postmodernity has initiated renewed sociological examination of culture and identity.

CULTURE, IDENTITY AND CONSUMERISM

Consumerism is a key aspect of contemporary society, and is seen as playing an important role in the formation of self-identity. **Robert Bocock** has suggested that the role of consumption has been greatly neglected by sociologists, largely because of the belief that to focus on consumption tends to lead to a neglect of political issues such as poverty and inequality. However, as Bocock points out, consumption and our ability to buy certain products does affect all members of society, even those whose lack of wealth means that they are frequently excluded from full participation in society.

Bocock creates a convincing case for suggesting that our consumer choices are a crucial part of cultural life. This becomes particularly apparent when culture is defined in terms of symbolic values and meanings. The clothes and food which we buy can be an important indicator of our social position and status. Consumption can also reflect a person's self-image, or make a statement about an identity someone aspires to. Bocock draws this idea from the work of **Thorstein Veblen** who used the term 'conspicuous consumption' to refer to the tactical consumption of the aspiring social classes, who wished to emulate the aristocracy and aspired to high status.

For postmodernist sociologists such as Baudrillard, the pressure to consume is a phenomenon created by the mass media. In the account of contemporary society given by Baudrillard, an individual's identity is no longer formed predominantly by class, ethnicity or gender. Baudrillard sees contemporary society as dominated by the mass media. It is information and images which we gain from the media which have the greatest influence upon our identity and our behaviour. Baudrillard sees people in contemporary society as living in an environment which is media 'saturated'. It is impossible to escape the influence of mass media. For Baudrillard, this is clearly a bad thing, since the result is that we can no longer tell the difference between reality and television; television has become our reality. Baudrillard uses the term 'seduced' to describe the way the media creates desires within viewers. The end result of this postmodern, media saturated culture however, is that identity is fluid; we can become who we wish, simply by purchasing the 'correct' clothes, accessories, etc., which will represent our preferred identity.

WHAT IS THE ROLE OF THE SHOPPING PRECINCT?

OTHER STUDIES OF IDENTITY AND CONSUMERISM

Sociologists such as **Frank Mort** and **Sean Nixon**, take a more cautious view of the idea that identity is completely mouldable according to the wishes of the individual.

New man

Frank Mort's study of consumerism has examined shifts in cultural expressions of masculinity, particularly focusing on the uses advertisers and others made of the concept of the 'new man' phenomenon of the 1980s to the mid 1990s. According to sociologist Sean Nixon the idea of the new man can be traced back to the release of one particular advertisement in late 1985, 'Launderette', which featured the model Nick Kamen and music by Marvin Gaye. The advert was used to promote Levi jeans. Frank Mort's study argues that the whole phenomenon of the new man marked an important moment in British cultural history, since it was a period which saw the sexualisation of men's bodies, and provided men with an alternative, indeed some would say, with several, alternative masculine identities. Up until this period, so the argument goes, the attitude of British males to the use of perfumes and various other toiletries had generally been a negative one. The use of subtle perfumes was generally seen as effeminate, in contrast to the attitude of men in other European cultures. However, Mort's study suggests that the change in cultural attitudes was not simply a passive acceptance of a new set of values invented by the manufacturers of perfumes and aftershave. Mort's study highlights the role of advertisers and a variety of style 'experts' and journalists in promoting and popularising a new consumer market and, in fact, in helping to create a new range of cultural identities.

New Man to New Lad

Sean Nixon's study covers much of the same territory, but is concerned to identify the role of commercial institutions in promoting, and indeed producing, various forms of culture. Nixon examines in detail how the notion of the new man was tied into a variety of marketing and selling techniques which rather than assuming that all young men were the same, and indeed, were new men in the same way, carefully altered the image of the new man according to factors such as social class. Nixon compares the style of different retailers aiming to attract different consumers. Thus Nixon sees the retail chain Next as appealing to the young service class professional, Paul Smith marketing itself by trying to create a sense of upper class exclusiveness and Top Man pitching for the stylish casual lad. As Nixon notes, the 1980s retail boom saw retailers paying much more attention to shop design in an attempt to lure consumers. Image has been all important in this task, with shops attempting to create a strong visual impression, selling not simply goods, but the image of a lifestyle. The activities of retailers give a practical demonstration of the idea that through consuming we are creating a sense of identity. A key point for Nixon is that the new man imagery of the 1980s made it possible for a display of male sensuality and narcissism. For the first time in British culture, it became acceptable for men to look, indeed, almost to stare, at other men's bodies in various degrees of exposure. Thus style magazines and shops would display pictures of naked male torsos. Nixon also describes how men's clothing retailers designed shop spaces which actively encouraged the display of the male body, and encouraged men to look at themselves and each other, without danger of criticism.

Nixon argues that masculinity in Western cultures can be seen as defined in contrast to femininity; thus any aspects of behaviour which are seen as feminine may be defined as taboo for men. Nixon suggests that the phenomena of the 1980s new man acted so as to loosen the cultural opposition between gay and straight masculine identities. Masculine identity became, for a short time, a little ambiguous. However, Nixon suggests that throughout this period there were strong continuities with more traditional conceptualisations of male identity. Thus, Nixon argues, it is no surprise to observe the rise in the 1990s of the 'new lad' and 'new laddism'. This can be seen as being represented through television programmes such as *Men Behaving Badly, This Life, Friends, They Think It's All Over, Fantasy Football League,* magazines such as *Loaded,* and *GQ,* and perhaps books like Nick Hornby's *Fever Pitch* and all of Martin Amis's novels to date.

Study point

- Consider the possibility that the concept of the 'new man' is a media myth.

McDONALDISATION — BURGER CULTURE AND RISK SOCIETY?

An alternative view of contemporary society stresses the contribution made by the German sociologist **Max Weber**. According to Max Weber one of the key cultural values encouraged by the development of capitalism is that of rationality. For Weber, capitalism leads to an increasingly rationalised culture. By rationalisation, Weber meant to refer to the way in which the behaviour of individuals and institutions becomes increasingly calculated or planned. This is also called instrumentalism. Weber is highly critical of rationalisation, arguing that it leads to a society where increasingly values are left unquestioned. Weber explains that this occurs because rationalisation is such a powerful means of organising institutions and societies. The ability to organise and achieve goals quickly starts to take precedence over examining the value and the worthiness of the goals themselves. Weber described the modern world as 'disenchanted', since all relationships became dominated by the need to subject all our behaviour and social life to rationalisation and the ability to calculate the predicted results of any particular action.

The concerns identified by Max Weber are reflected in two recent pieces of sociological work by **George Ritzer** and **Ulrich Beck**.

George Ritzer's book, *The McDonaldisation of Society*, takes up Weber's idea of rationalisation, and argues that we live in a society whose institutions have been subjected to a continuous and radical process of rationalisation. McDonald's have created a worldwide business which now allows us to buy an identical fast food product just about anywhere in the world. The process by which McDonald's products are made, and indeed the way in which they are sold and the style of the McDonald's restaurant, are identical, regardless of which country the outlet is situated in. It is possible to order a meal in a McDonald's restaurant in France or Russia even if one does not speak French or Russian – 'Big Mac' sounds about the same in every language, although as the character played by John Travolta in the film *Pulp Fiction* notes, there can be a few exceptions to this broad picture.

On first reflection, it could be suggested that Ritzer's concept of McDonaldisation is more descriptive of modern society than postmodernism, since it is concerned with the mass production of standardised goods. It has previously been noted that postmodernists tend to suggest that postmodern society is one in which there is a shift away from mass production to so-called 'small batch production'; the production of specialised goods and products for niche markets. Ritzer is himself critical of many aspects of the postmodernist view of contemporary society. However, there is much in Ritzer's account which can compliment postmodernist theory.

Globalisation is perhaps one of the most obvious ways in which the idea of McDonaldisation compliments postmodernism. As Ritzer points out, McDonald's is a global business, with retail outlets all over the world. In this sense McDonald's, like many other large business corporations, helps to promote a global culture in many different societies, each with their own indigenous culture. Moreover, postmodernists could point to the ways in which McDonald's exemplifies consumer culture. Retail outlets such as McDonald's provide an environment which enable customers to create a certain identity; arguably McDonald's is classless, young, affluent and up to date. Moreover, postmodernists could suggest that since McDonald's is now one of many alternative fast food retailers, contemporary society can be seen as offering the eager consumer a variety of different images and identities to choose from.

RISK SOCIETY AND NEW SOCIAL MOVEMENTS

The contemporary German sociologist Ulrich Beck has offered another view of contemporary society, which also uses the idea of rationalisation. Beck's book *The Risk Society*, argues that contemporary industrial societies have indeed undergone considerable social change in recent years. Beck argues that the most important aspect of these changes has been that issues of inequality are now of lesser importance. He argues that what is of greater importance in contemporary society is the increasing degree of risk which technology brings to our lives.

Beck has been particularly interested in environmental issues, and wishes to draw attention to the dangers of pollution, the possibility of nuclear catastrophe, and the periodic appearance of diseases such as AIDS or BSE. These are all problems which are 'man-made'. Beck also points out that the scale of these risks is now global – a nuclear disaster in Russia will affect people all over Europe, the destruction of the ozone layer has effects on the world climate, not just Western Europe and the USA. One of Beck's key points about these issues however, is that they are all very difficult, if not impossible, for us to control.

Beck argues that these changes in society lead to cultural changes. People in contemporary society are less likely to be attracted to formal party politics, and more likely to find appeal in a variety of new social movements, focusing on particular single issues. Since people can no longer gain a sense of security from the 'old' sources such as class or community, they may have to create new ways of gaining a sense of identity. Frequently, Beck argues, this may come from a much wider variety of sources than was the case in modern society. An example here would be the increasing popularity of the Green movement or New Age travellers. Such movements can be seen as being based not on class, but on a belief in a particular form of lifestyle, and they will recruit members from a wide range of social groups. Thus contemporary society is characterised by a different culture, one where risk is an accepted and acknowledged aspect of life and, moreover, is now seen as the key aspect of social existence. This in turn has effects upon the range of cultural identities which are available to those living in contemporary society. Like postmodernists, Beck sees individuals as being much freer to create a sense of identity than modernist sociologists would previously have suggested was possible.

Study point

- Consider the areas of greatest risk in your own life. Are these greater than those of previous generations or just different types of risk?

MANAGEMENT CULTURE

Many sociologists have been interested in the rise of so-called 'management culture', which has been noted in both the business world and in public services such as education and the health service. Management experts or 'gurus' have been a notable feature of contemporary work. These experts have argued that employers have to motivate their staff more effectively in order to increase business efficiency, competitiveness and profitability. This is seen as another aspect of globalisation, since competition becomes more intense in a global economy. As a result of these views, businesses and public sector services have been urged to adopt a variety of practices to increase efficiency and to make staff more involved in the business.

WORK AND IDENTITY

In practical terms, management culture has thus had the effect of spawning a variety of schemes attempting to increase worker involvement and identification with employing organisations. These range from Japanese style 'quality circles' which encourage and reward workers' ideas to improve efficiency, to the Investors in People Award (IIP) promoted through government agencies in Britain. IIP aims to encourage employers to promote the training and development of employees, on the basis that doing so will aid the competitiveness of business and public service organisations. Such measures are typical of 'management culture'. Management culture has also ushered in a new vocabulary, using terms such as 'mission statement', 'quality', 'customer service'. **Paul du Gay** and **Graeme Salaman** argue that such terms have an important influence on the cultural identity of employees, helping to create what they call an 'entrepreneurial culture'. Employees are encouraged to 'think of themselves as being like a business', and thus are required to plan 'personal development' with the aim of improving their performance ('adding value') at work. In terms of identity, this of course means that people are being asked to invest even more of their personality and emotional energy in their work. Employers who take this approach are in fact demanding considerable commitment; it is becoming increasingly difficult to separate one's work identity from home identity, or the public and the private.

Those who are critical of the development of management culture point out that all these developments are occurring at a time when, precisely as a result of intense global economic competition, businesses are less likely to be able to offer guarantees of lifelong employment in return for loyalty. Thus some sociologists would argue that in reality management culture is little more than a new technique for the control of the workforce.

Study point
• The new management culture encourages people to work more efficiently for companies. Are there ways in which a new educational culture could develop similar attitudes amongst students?

THE INFORMATION SOCIETY?

Jean-Francois Lyotard has argued that one aspect of postmodern society is the proliferation of information, partly as a result of the development of computer technology. The ability to pass and access information easily is itself an aspect of globalisation. Lyotard argues however, that far from leading to a situation where information becomes accessible to all and can be used for the benefit of all, this leads to a situation where information is misused. Lyotard uses the term 'performativity' to indicate that information is used simplistically in many areas of social life. The use of statistical information by governments, business organisations, and the mass media, does not, Lyotard would argue, provide us with the truth, or better information. By the term 'performativity' Lyotard wishes to indicate that the goals and aims of services are in reality neglected. An example here would be education league tables, or health service performance indicators. Lyotard would argue that such statistical information shows us little about the reality of what goes on in education or the health service. Only those things which can be quantified or measured are seen as relevant.

Study point

- Suggest some arguments for and against the use of school/college/university league tables as indicators of their performance.

CYBERCULTURE

Closely related to Lyotard's discussion of the information society is the notion of cyberculture. Cyberculture refers to the culture which is growing up around computer technology ('cyber' means artificial). Although this is a very new area of study, it seems fairly clear that computer technology will have important social and cultural effects. Cyberculture can be usefully understood in the light of Baudrillard's concept of hyperreality. We are increasingly familiar with the term 'virtual reality', which translates loosely to meaning 'artificial reality'. The idea of virtual reality thus ties in very closely with Baudrillard's view of hyperreality, and the uncertainty that it implies we must have about the world we live in. As many computer afficionados have found, the computer does not simply put the world at your fingertips; it also enables you to adopt the identity of your choosing, hence the popularity of the internet for a new sort of computer dating, penfriends, and other e-mail interactions. Arguably these new forms of relationship pander to an individual's desire for control and autonomy, without having to go through the social processes of negotiation and compromise. Computer games such as 'Lara Croft' enable adolescent teenage boys to have a virtual relationship with a fantasy female character after which, it may be suggested, real females will seem a poor substitute. Thus cyberculture is changing the nature of human relationships; instant gratification is being taken to new levels.

Moreover the philosopher and social theorist **Sadie Plant** has argued that it is women who are particularly suited to cyberculture; they do not necessarily have to be seen as victims of technology. Whether cyberculture will be so female friendly is a matter for further research.

CONTEMPORARY SOCIETY AND CONTEMPORARY SOCIAL THEORY

Many sociologists are particularly unhappy with those postmodernists who are critical of 'grand theories', and who believe that it is not possible to achieve objective and unbiased sociological knowledge. Marxists such as **Alex Callinicos** have also been particularly critical of postmodernism, seeing it as ignoring the key aspect of contemporary society – its capitalist nature. For those such as Callinicos this means that, fundamentally, contemporary society in the late twentieth century is little different to society in the middle of the twentieth century.

However, others influenced by Marxism have been more flexible in their assessment. **David Harvey** has argued that from the 1970s capitalism has changed in significant ways. Harvey has studied the development of post-Fordism – the change from mass production to flexible production – and the way this has occurred in a global context. Harvey has particularly focused upon the way that contemporary culture is the result of the development of new ways of organising finance and trading.

Harvey is clear that cultural changes have occurred, but sees these changes as part and parcel of a capitalist economy. In this sense, Harvey's concerns are similar to those of the Marxist cultural critic, **Frederic Jameson**. Jameson modifies the claims of postmodernist theory, suggesting that what has occurred in the last part of the twentieth century is that culture has become commodified (see Chapter 4). In adopting the concept of commodification, Jameson remains within the realms of traditional Marxist theory. However, Jameson modifies this, by arguing that in what he calls late capitalism the commodification of culture has seen culture become part of the economic system. Thus Jameson argues that:

- Base and superstructure, or culture and economy, are becoming much more closely tied together.
- Culture in late capitalist society simply reflects the economic logic of the current stage of capitalism. There is a need for continually novel goods and services – hence, niche markets.

- Culture, rather than simply reflecting the means of production, has itself become a product. Thus, there is now a thriving business sector concentrating on the so-called 'culture industry', which includes fashion, music, theatre, television and the film industry

Jameson argues, that what some term postmodernism is simply the latest manifestation of culture within capitalist society.

Activity
Visit a range of shops in your locality and note the extent of 'novelty' goods. Which ones are tied into major advertising campaigns on TV or are associated with films or CDs? Is there evidence to support the idea of a new 'culture industry'?

Both Harvey and Jameson argue that contemporary societies are experiencing tremendous social change. Harvey and Jameson however, would argue that the current period is best thought of as 'late capitalism', since the economic systems and structures of capitalism are still key social institutions. Harvey and Jameson's work suggests that without adequate analysis of these institutions, sociological studies will fail to help us understand contemporary society.

ANTHONY GIDDENS AND LATE MODERNITY

Anthony Giddens is another sociologist who has taken a critical approach to the claims of postmodernism, whilst wanting to insist that contemporary society is indeed experiencing tremendous social change. Giddens rejects the theoretical aspects of postmodernism which suggest that objectivity and 'grand' theories are unworkable, but maintains that the effects of globalisation have transformed contemporary society and culture. Giddens echoes the views of Harvey to some extent, arguing that globalisation has indeed speeded up the pace of change and of contemporary life.

However, Giddens has much to say about the consequences of these changes for our individual lives. In terms of culture (both definitions), Giddens argues that contemporary societies do tend to promote a global and cosmopolitan culture and lifestyle. In this respect, Giddens argues that our society can helpfully be thought of as a post-traditional society, since tradition of all types is increasingly challenged, simply as a result of the way in which individuals are bombarded with alternative lifestyles in contemporary society. It follows that individual identity is constructed in different ways to traditional society, where an individual's sense of identity was largely predetermined by, for example, their class, age, gender or ethnic status.

Giddens refers to the way in which the process by which we create our self-identity becomes a 'reflexive project'. By this Giddens simply means that we are able to monitor our progress in achieving the sort of self-image to which we aspire. Individual's can assess how successful they are in creating their desired identity, and if they fall short of it, they may adopt various strategies to tackle this problem, such as dieting, going on a course, buying a new set of clothes and so on.

Study point

- Consider the extent to which you have consciously established an identity and lifestyle, rather than have one imposed upon you. To what extent do your cultural values and outlook differ from those of your parents or other generations? Consider issues of dress; leisure; tastes in entertainment and voting intentions.

Giddens has argued that in contemporary society we have witnessed the rise to prominence of the 'pure relationship'. Giddens means by this term to refer to the way intimate relationships have changed, a process he describes in his book *The Transformation of Intimacy*. Giddens argues that our personal relationships are no longer bound by economic need, as was common in pre-industrial society. Giddens claims that individuals are now free to initiate personal relationships on a 'pure' basis, that is on the basis of personal and emotional factors, such as 'falling in love' with the partner of their choice. Unlike Jameson and Harvey, Giddens prefers to refer to the contemporary era as 'late modernity', rather than late capitalism or postmodernism. Giddens argues that whilst the processes and trends of modern life have speeded up, there has been no fundamental structural change warranting a new name. Giddens rejects the term 'late capitalism', since capitalism is only one aspect of modern societies. In Giddens' view, it is also important to note that modern societies involve industrialism (the technology of production), administrative systems (bureaucracies) and military power.

Study point

- List some of the major features of modern society which remain largely unchanged over time.

All of the sociologists discussed above have doubts about some aspects of postmodernist theory, but have found it useful to some extent in identifying the nature of social change in contemporary society. It is now appropriate to evaluate the claims of postmodernist theory.

EVALUATION OF POSTMODERNISM

Whatever its faults, postmodernism has certainly enlivened sociological debate. There are many criticisms made of the theory, the most important of which will now be discussed.

CRITICISMS OF POSTMODERNISM

It exaggerates the scale of social change
- It can be suggested that postmodernism exaggerates when it claims that cultural distinctions are blurred, and that there is a global culture.
- Cultural critics argue that differences between high and popular culture have always been blurred and contested, and opinions on such issues are always subject to changes in fashion.
- Culture is not a static concept, and ideas on culture are subject to continual change.
- Cultural tastes are still very much influenced by class, ethnicity and gender.
- In terms of the idea of a global culture, it can be argued that despite some evidence of homogenisation, what is more striking is the variety of cultural adaptation and change across different societies.
- It can be suggested that postmodernism gives unjustified prominence to the role of the mass media in society, at the expense of economic structures.

It is voluntaristic
- It appears to imply that human beings are free to act as they wish, and are not impeded by social structures such as class, ethnicity or gender.
- Postmodernism often implies that individuals can freely choose the sort of identity they wish to create for themselves, regardless of social divisions and stratification systems.
- Culture tends to encourage and privilege certain conceptions of masculinity and femininity, as well as ethnicity and various age groups.

It is relativistic
Postmodernists' most well known theoretical claim, the disbelief in grand theory, or metanarratives (theories which seek to explain everything), has also led to considerable debate.

- Lyotard's claim, put simply, means that it is not possible for sociologists (or anyone else) to be objective or to gain absolute truth, and leads logically to what is called 'relativism'.
- Relativism means that no one theory can rightfully claim to be the truth. If this is the case then it follows that all theories are basically of equal worth, and the only basis upon which to discriminate between different theories is presumably personal choice. This is in stark contrast to the aims of modernist sociology, much of which aspired to scientific status.

It is politically conservative

- Postmodernism can be seen as a pessimistic theory which suggests that it does not matter what we think or whether we are right or wrong.

- Postmodernism may appear to be implying that we give up bothering about right and wrong, since we will never be able to prove its truth. As such, many see it as 'conservative', in that it may lead individuals to adopt a position of indifference or apathy to the truth.

DEFENCES OF POSTMODERNISM

Several points may be made in defence of postmodernism.

- Firstly, it is important in evaluating postmodernism to note that there are several critical interpretations which can be made of the basic theory. Many sociologists are now drawing upon and using postmodernist concepts; this does not mean that they have to accept all of the theoretical suppositions of postmodernism.

- It can be argued that postmodernism has tapped into some important areas of social change in a new and fruitful way. Postmodernists focus upon the subtleties and complexities of social processes, and their criticism of the overgeneralising aspects of modernist sociology has been particularly useful. This has encouraged sociologists to reconceptualise gender, ethnicity and class, and to examine more closely the ways in which these are culturally constructed, and indeed the active way in which individuals attempt to construct their identity within the constraints allowed by social structures.

- In doing this, postmodernism has forced sociologists to acknowledge a greater degree of complexity in social life, and to avoid reductionism and essentialism. The term reductionism refers to the belief that sociological explanations can be reduced to one key aspect of social structure. Essentialism refers to the idea that a concept such as gender, class or ethnicity can be defined in terms of a simple and undisputed essence, eg the 'essential' female will be caring and emotional.

- Finally it can be agreed that there are indeed many problems with relativism, full discussion of which would go beyond the scope of this book. Nevertheless the criticique of the modernist belief that objectivity and truth can be attained through the use of scientific method, has at least been useful in moderating the tendency to make sociological over-generalisations. As many feminists and black sociologists would argue, modernist sociology has often denied them a voice, and has failed to tell their story.

SUMMARY

Sociology has always been a subject which involves debate. The debates between modernists and postmodernists, whatever else they have done for, or to, the subject, illustrate that it is very much a live and relevant discipline. Sociology needs to examine culture, identity, and concepts such as class and the structures which late capitalist societies create and maintain. In doing this, sociology will continue to have much of relevance to say in a rapidly changing society, and be able to show us how our own lives are shaped by larger social forces.

Group Work

1 Create an evaluation chart (see introduction) to summarise the postmodernist analysis of contemporary society. Produce a brief conclusion stating your group view as to the usefulness of postmodernist theory.
2 Debate the following motions, 'Concepts such as class, ethnicity and gender, have little influence upon individual identity in contemporary society. There is little need for sociologists to spend so much time discussing these outdated concepts.'

Practice Questions

ITEM A

Keith watched a very great deal of TV, always had done, years and years of it, aeons of TV. Boy, did Keith burn that tube. And that tube burnt him, nuked him, its cathodes crackling like cancer. 'TV,' he thought, or 'Modern Reality' or 'The World'. It was the world of TV that told him what the world was. How does all the TV time work on a modern person, a person like Keith? The fact that he would have passed up a visit to the Louvre or the Prado in favour of ten minutes alone with a knicker catalogue – this, perhaps, was a personal quirk. But TV came at Keith like it came at everybody else; and he had nothing whatever to keep it out. He couldn't grade or filter it. So he thought TV was real..[...] Not an active reality, like, say, darts, on which the camera obligingly spied and eavesdropped. No, an exemplary reality, all beautifully and gracefully interconnected, where nothing hurt much and nobody got old. It was a high trapeze, the artists all sequin and tutu (look at that bird!), enacted far above the sawdust, the peanut shells and poodle droppings, up there, beyond a taut a twanging safety-net called money.

From London Fields, by Martin Amis, Penguin, 1989, p55

ITEM B

There was this Englishman who worked in the London office of a multinational corporation based in the United States. He drove home one evening in his Japanese car. His wife, who worked in a firm which imported German kitchen equipment, was already at home. Her small Italian car was often quicker through the traffic. After a meal which included New Zealand lamb, Californian carrots, Mexican honey, French cheese and Spanish wine, they settled down to watch a programme on their television set, which had been made in Finland. The programme was a retrospective celebration of the war to capture the Falkland Islands. As they watched it they felt warmly patriotic, and very proud to be British.

Raymond Williams, Towards 2000, Chatto and Windus, 1983, p177

1 Explain why the view of contemporary society described in Item A could be described as postmodern. (4)

2 Identify three criticims which are made of the idea that contemporary society has entered a new and distinct era. (3)

3 Identify the concept which has been used to explain the phenomenon described in Item B. (1)

4 Using information from the Items and elsewhere, evaluate the view that contemporary society is witnessing the development of a global culture. (9)

5 Evaluate the usefulness of postmodernist theory for understanding culture and identity in contemporary society. (8)

Coursework

1 Undertake a study to test the hypothesis that increasing consumption leads to a neglect of political issues, such as poverty and inequality.

2 Undertake a study to test the views of Beck that people in contemporary society are less attracted by formal party politics than by new social movements which focus on single issues, such as animal rights.

3 Write a detailed mission statement which claims to promote new positive attitudes in students towards their work and which results in greater levels of success. Undertake an observational study to monitor the response of students who read it; note their views and gain from them ideas they would like to add or remove from it.

SELECTED REFERENCES

Ahmad, W. I. V. (1992) 'The maligned healer: the 'hakim' and western medicine', *New Community*, 18 (4), pp 521–536.

Bauman, Z. (1990) *Thinking Sociologically*, Oxford, Blackwells.

Beardsworth, A., & Keil, T. (1993) 'Hungry for knowledge? The sociology of food and eating', *Sociology Review*, Vol 3, No 2, pp 11–17.

Becker, H. (1963) *Outsiders*, New York, The Free Press.

Bocock, R. (1993) *Consumption*, London, Routledge.

Canaan, J. (1996) 'One thing leads to another: drinking, fighting and working-class masculinities', in Mac an Ghaill (1996).

Chignell, H., & Abbott, D. (1995) 'An Interview with Anthony Giddens', *Sociology Review*, Vol 5, No 2, pp 10–14.

Connell, R. (1995) *Masculinities*, Cambridge, Polity.

Drury, B. (1991) 'Sikh girls and the maintenance of an ethnic culture', *New Community*, Vol 17, No 3, pp 387–99.

Duncombe, J., & Marsden, D. (1995) '"Workaholics" and "whingeing women": theorising intimacy and emotion work – the last frontier of gender inequality?', *The Sociological Review*, Vol 43, No 1, February, pp 150–169.

Dworkin, A. (1981) *Pornography: Men Possessing Women*, New York, Perigee.

Giddens, A. (1989) *The Consequences of Modernity*, Cambridge, Polity.

Goffman, E. (1961) *Asylums*, Harmondsworth, Penguin.

Haywood, C., & Mac an Ghaill, M. (1996) '*Schooling masculinities*', in Mac an Ghaill (1996).

Hill, R. A. (1987) 'The Housing Characteristics and Aspirations of Leicester's Inner City Asian Community', unpublished Ph.D. University of Leicester.

Hockey, J., & James, A. (1993) *Growing Up and Growing Old – Ageing and Dependency in the Life Course*, London, Sage.

Hoggart, R. (1957) *The Uses of Literacy*, Harmondsworth, Penguin.

Jorgensen, N., et al. (1997) *Sociology An Interactive Approach*, London, Collins Educational.

King, A. (1997) 'The Lads: masculinity and the new consumption of football', *Sociology*, Vol 31, No 2, pp 329–346.

Kirby, M., et al.(1997) *Sociology in Perspective*, Oxford, Heinemann.

Lenskyj (1986) *Out of Bounds: Women, Sport and Sexuality*, Toronto, Women's Press.

Mac an Ghaill, M. (1996) 'What about the boys?': schooling, class and crisis masculinity', *The Sociological Review*, Vol 44, No 3, pp 381–395.

Mac an Ghaill, M. (ed) (1996) *Understanding Masculinities*, Buckingham, Open University Press.

MacKinnon, C. (1989) *Toward a Feminist Theory of the State*, Cambridge Mass., Harvard University Press.

Majors, R. (1990) 'Cool pose: black masculinity and sports', in M. A. Messner and D. F. Sabo (eds) *Sport, Men and the Gender Order*, Champaign Illinois, USA, Human Kinetics.

Marquand, D. (1995) 'After Whig imperialism: can there be a new British identity?', *New Community*, 21 (2) pp 183–193.

Modood, T. (1988) 'Black racial equality and Asian Identity', *New Community*, 14 (3), pp 397–404.

Modood, T. (1990) 'Catching up with Jesse Jackson: on being oppressed and being somebody', *New Community*, 17 (1) , pp 85-96.

Modood, T. (1990) 'British Asian Muslims and the Salman Rushdie affair', *Political Quarterly*, 61 (20), pp 143–60.

Nixon, S. (1996) *Hard Looks*, London, UCL Press.

O'Donnell, M. (1997) *Introduction to Sociology*, 4th edition, Walton on Thames, Nelson ITP.

Orbach, S. (1986) *Fat is a Feminist Issue*, Arrow Books.

Parker, A. (1996) 'Sporting masculinities: gender relations and the body', in Mac an Ghaill (1996).

Pilcher, J. (1995) 'Growing up and growing older – the sociology of age', *Sociology Review*, September pp 8–13.

Plant, S. (1997) *Zeros and Ones: Digital Women and The New Technoculture*, London, Fourth Estate.

Scott, J. (1993) *Who Rules Britain?*, Cambridge, Polity.

Scully, J. (1997) 'A "stage Irish identity"– an example of "symbolic power"', *New Community*, 23 (3) pp 385–398.

Shakespeare, T. (1995) 'Back to the future? New Genetics and disabled people', *Critical Social Policy*, No 44/45, Autumn, pp 22–35.

Shakespeare, T. (1994) 'Disabled People: dustbins for disavowal?' *Disability and Society*, Vol 9, No 3, pp 283–299.

Small, S. (1991) 'Racialised relations in Liverpool: A contemporary anomaly', *New Community*, 17 (4), pp 511–37.

Small, S. (1993) 'Key Thinkers – William du Bois', *Sociology Review*, Vol 3, No 1, pp 15–16.

Song, M. (1997) '"You're becoming more and more English": investigating Chinese siblings' cultural identities', *New Community* 23 (3) pp 343-362.

Strinati, D. (1995) *An Introduction to Theories of Popular Culture*, London, Routledge.

Turner, G. (1996) *British Cultural Studies -- An Introduction*, London, Routledge.

Walby, S. (1990) *Theorising Patriarchy*, Cambridge, Polity.

Wolff, J. (1990) *Feminine Sentences*, Cambridge, Polity.

FURTHER SOURCES OF INFORMATION

The magazine *Sociology Review*, published four times a year by Philip Allan Ltd, contains a variety of useful topical articles on issues of sociological interest.

WEB SITES

Those with access to the Internet and World Wide Web can access a huge range of information. The following sites are well worth checking. Those looking for specific material on culture and identity may find using a good search engine (such as yahoo – see below) and key words to be a useful strategy.

Social Science 'Index' on http://www.yahoo.com/

Electronic Journal of Sociology on http://gpu.srv.ualberta.ca.8010/home1.html

The Postmodern Adventure on http://ccwf.cc.utexas.edu/~panicbuy/HaTeMail/marxtopomo.htm

ATSS on http://www.le.ac.uk/education/centres/ATSS/atss.html

A useful guide for further information is *The Internet and World Wide Web Rough Guide* by Angus J. Kennedy.

ATSS

The Association for the Teaching of the Social Sciences (ATSS), publishes the journal *Social Science Teacher* and produces a variety of other resources for sociology teachers. For further information contact: ATSS, P.O. Box 61, Watford WD2 2NH.

INDEX